GODS OF COMMERCE

HOW BUSINESS REALLY WORKS

OTHER BOOKS BY MICHAEL PHILLIPS

Disarming Anti-Japanese Prejudice
Clear Glass Press

Marketing Without Advertising
Nolo Press (with Salli Rasberry)

Honest Business
Random House and Shambhala Classics (with Salli Rasberry)

The Seven Laws of Money
Random House and Shambhala Classics (with Salli Rasberry)

Simple Living Investments
Clear Glass Press (with Catherine Campbell)

GODS OF COMMERCE

HOW BUSINESS REALLY WORKS

by Michael Phillips

Clear Glass Press
San Francisco

Michael Phillips (1938–)
Library of Congress Catalog Card Number 96-96518
ISBN 0931425-03-4

For individual orders of Gods of Commerce, call 800-372-4238,
Access Code #10
To order on the World Wide Web: www.well.com/user/mp/books.html
Bookstores: Order from Bookpeople, Oakland, California 800-999-4650
10 9 8 7 6 5 4 3 2

Dedicated to
Sonya M. Richardson

CONTENTS

Foreword, ix

Introduction, xi

Chapter 1: The Big Three, 1

Chapter 2: Urbanus, God of Trade, 5

Chapter 3: Ganesh, God of Industry, 23

Chapter 4: Honestas, Goddess of Clientry, 61

Epilogue, 103

Bibliography, 111

Glossary, 113

Index, 115

About the Author, 117

FOREWORD

A few years ago Michael Phillips gave me an early memorandum draft of some of his recent thinking about the changing nature of business in the U.S.

In it, he compared what he called "Trade" with "Industry" against something he termed "Clientry."

Phillips observed that "Trade" was an ancient form of commerce. It consisted of a product offering, an allowance for overhead and profit and a price. Trade, he said, takes place anywhere and everywhere. In the jungle and in prisons.

Industry, however, depends upon large markets of buyers so that economies of scale in manufacturing can be achieved. Mass markets depend upon social and technical stability to allow business conventions to arise and product planning to take place.

Clientry, by contrast, seems more narrowly circumscribed to Phillips—more self-contained, more dependent upon repeat business—like a medical practice, for example. One has clients whom one comes to know and identify. Such a relationship is free from the hazards of social instability and technical change—as long as the supplier pays intimate attention to client needs.

Phillips' identification of "Clientry" seemed particularly relevant to my business—the SL Corporation (Sherrill-Lubinski). The SL Corporation is a leading developer of tools for creating animated graphical interfaces for complex computer-control systems—like those interactive, animated computer screens that control and monitor nuclear power plants, telephone networks or satellite control systems.

The SL Corporation designs and manufactures the computer graphics tools to build these interfaces. Therefore, you might say, SL Corporation has developed and maintains a vital technology for companies whose own technology is itself very complex. These companies operate in "mission critical" situations where lives may be at stake. Our customers are usually the large technical firms who seek out the best available technology: General Electric, Toshiba, Motorola, ABB Bovari, for example.

Our commercial relations with our clients must be genuine, mutually beneficial and, most of all, closely involved. Our technology must work perfectly with theirs.

The software business is always changing and there is always great migration and volatility in the marketplace. It is a situation that seemed perfect as an application for the Phillips "client-centered" business. In analyzing our sales I was struck by the high percentage of repeat business from existing customers.

As a result I abstracted Phillips' draft and delivered much of its thinking to the staff at company lunch meetings, along with a separately circulated reprint.

Since then our lives have become simpler because we are now beating the right bushes. We no longer despair that we do not have stable markets like manufacturing. We form close alliances with our customer-clients and take next steps in product development together as often as we can. We try not to scratch our heads in public, but we feel no need to hide our doubts about the future during obviously confusing times.

We try to be ready to jump in the right direction when clarity strikes.

Dr. Peter N. Sherrill, CEO, SL Corporation, January 1997
(Dr. Sherrill 1926- April 1997)

INTRODUCTION

There is no single theory of business. There is, however, a broad view of business that can be helpful in understanding the nature of commerce and in making business decisions.

Most business owners and corporate CEOs do not possess business school degrees or a theory of business. Instead they have a good sense of logic and a foundation of knowledge that allows them to be effective in operating a business. Among many of the businesspeople I've worked with, however, there is a common belief that *other* businesspeople have a theory of business. The popular book *What They Don't Teach at Harvard Business School* (Bantam Doubleday Dell Publishers 1988) may have sold so well because it promised to explain business to people who think there is a theory to be learned.

People who have gone to business school do not have this same view. They know there is no theory of business. What most of them learned from several years of reading business literature and associating with professors and fellow business students is that there are no abstract concepts of business. Schooling provides skills rather than theory—skills such as analyzing financial statements and dealing with the legal realm of business practice. In addition, business students learn useful anecdotes, practice dealing with complex business situations, and learn the technical language of business operations. Together, these experiences afford some degree of confidence in daily business life.

Business is pragmatic, not theoretical. It grows out of world views, not theories. It is my contention, in this book, that global commerce is driven by the unexpressed world views of millions of businesspeople. These views are different from the views of non-commercial people. There are as many as ten world views of business that can guide successful businesspeople; some have only a few of these views, while others may have all ten. There is a progression among the views from those developed early in history to the more recent. The earliest world views created trade, while later views expanded it to a global industrial scale. Today, more recent views are bringing about new changes.

By "a business world view," I mean something as simple as the way of looking at business expressed by the statement "Let me look at your financial data to see whether you're doing a good job." It is a specific way of looking at certain facts and deciding what they mean. This way of interpreting facts is typical of businesspeople, who have a confidence in the way they see the world that is very different from the attitude of non-businesspeople.

The social forces acting on business internationally over long periods of time have not been the subject of much examination. This is slowly being remedied by the work of Alfred Chandler, Jr., Thomas Hughes, Mancur Olson, Joe Corn, Mary Douglas, James Beniger, and others in academia. I owe them all a debt of gratitude for helping me to formulate my ideas about business.

Nature and Commerce

I am indebted to Paul Hawken, who wrote a book called *The Ecology of Commerce*, for introducing me to the concept of ecology as a way of looking at business. I see commerce as a medium almost as pervasive as nature. It is a medium in which humankind is immersed and which we have created, and which determines much about the way we live our lives.

The ecology of commerce is evident on a walk through the neighborhoods of San Francisco. In the pristine residential streets of wealthy Pacific Heights, commerce, for example, is invisible. In other residential blocks, many windows display United Parcel

Service pickup signs and autos have product and business logos. In Chinatown, apartments are found upstairs over shops. The Castro and the Haight-Ashbury districts have a mix of businesses, cafes, apartments, and houses run and occupied by a new generation of business and home owners. Each neighborhood is a different commercial niche, reflecting the people who nest, shop and eat there.

Economic Theories

My thinking about business was also influenced by my experiences in India, where I met businesspeople and learned about the elephant god Ganesh. My other influences include Max Weber and his book *Protestant Ethic and the Rise of Capitalism,* as well as his studies of Hinduism, Buddhism, Islam, Taoism, and Confucianism.

During the twentieth century, most thinking about business was in the thrall of a German who developed his theory writing in the British Museum in the 1860s. Karl Marx may not seem like a business intellectual, but his ideas of petite bourgeois values, imperialism, capitalism, monopoly, and profit motivation are the foundation of modern economics and business. Remove Marx's European concerns about class struggle and you have the intellectual framework on which most business thinking has been erected. It is to Marx that the concept of capitalism owes its linguistic power and political influence.

This book examines a system of business that was prevalent during Marx's time and which he called *petite bourgeois.* Today we understand it as trade. *Gods of Commerce* examines the edifice of industrialism that was just emerging in Marx's time and was the basis for Marxist theory. Finally, *Gods of Commerce* explores clientrism, a key idea that incorporates practices that are very different from the industrial practices of the last century.

Business and Culture

In my travels, I have found that different cultures have different degrees of business skill. In India I found a variety of business regions. Some regions were lush with open-air markets, shops, factories and small entrepreneurs scurrying everywhere. Others were devoid of nearly all commerce except farming and begging.

In West Africa, some tribes, like the Senegalese Fulani, are aggressive traders. Tribes in Mali, on the other hand, are purely agrarian. In Denmark and the Smarland region of Sweden (where Danes settled a millennium ago), small businesses thrive in every nook and cranny, while in some suburbs of Stockholm, building complexes house five thousand people without a single shop for miles. In downtown Moscow in the early 1980s, I could walk for an hour without seeing any sign of commerce. Getting off a plane the next day in a rural village of a few hundred settled farmers in Japan, I found more than one business for every two adults, including cigarette and candy shops in the corner windows of residences on the village road.

The differing cultural proclivities for business are well described by Thomas Sowell in his book *Race and Culture.* He describes many ethnic groups who migrated to new countries and succeeded in commerce, despite adverse conditions and prejudice, by using a high rate of saving, intense devotion to education, and mutual aid societies. This issue are discussed in *Gods of Commerce* because culture has much to do with a person's world views.

Max Weber, who lived in Germany during the late nineteenth and early twentieth century, was one of the originators of the field of sociology. He developed the theory that ideas and institutions are intimately related. His theory was partly based on the correlation he found between the success of Protestants in business in Germany at the turn of the twentieth century and their theology. Weber theorized that the Calvinist belief in predestination and the doctrine of the elect gave Protestants the confidence that they were meant to succeed in business.

I do not doubt the cultural propensity toward business; for me it is a given. I have witnessed widely differing ethnic propensities to succeed. I have seen my fellow Jews, for example, create businesses out of air, desert sand, and stone soup. I am also aware of the great individual variations within ethnic categories. My father was a failure at every one of his five different businesses, but my mother and my three brothers have done well in business.

Gods of Commerce examines three different ways of doing business, each organized around a different god of commerce, as well as the world views behind them and how actual businesses reflect these world views.

The Three Gods of Commerce

The three ways of doing business discussed in this book are personified by three gods: Urbanus, Ganesh, and Honestas. Ganesh is a reputable Indian elephant god featured in the literature and history of Hinduism; Urbanus and Honestas, however, are my creations. These "gods" are metaphorical concepts that I have used as an organizing principles in this book. They symbolize three distinct ways of looking at the world; in doing so they shed an archetypal light on a long tradition of worldwide business practices.

The three chapters based on the three gods examine how the world views of people in each of three business categories affect their ways of doing business, and also how the cultural background of businesspeople affects their business life.

Gods of Commerce is an attempt to look at the big picture of the world of business, to help put business matters into a meaningful perspective, and to examine how this way of thinking about business affects small business and the national economy. Following is an outline of three types of commerce discussed in this book and the associated world view that each god symbolizes.

CHAPTER ONE

THE BIG THREE

There are three forms of commerce: trade, industry and clientry.

The most impressive traders I have seen are the Fulani of West Africa. They have weekly open-air markets with tens of thousands of buyers and sellers. There is color, music, and enough excitement to make a trip on LSD seem mild. These markets probably long predated their discovery four centuries ago by the first Europeans to visit West Africa. A thousand years before that time, the earliest great traders were the Phoenicians, who carried on a prosperous naval trade throughout the Mediterranean.

The great industrialists emerged during the late 1800s. These men were most often of Nordic origin, with ancestors from Northern Germany, Scandinavia, the Netherlands, and Viking-settled Britain. Nearly all the great oil, steel, and chemical companies they founded still exist as major international industries.

The most impressive clientrists I have seen are the Japanese. They have more small businesses per capita than any other people, about twice the number of their closest competitors, the overseas Chinese, the French, and the Danes. Many Japanese ideas for retail business have shaped modern commerce.

To what can we attribute the differences of business propensities among cultures? In *The Seven Cultures of Capitalism,* Charles Hampden-Turner and his coauthor Alfons Trompenaars report their research on the significantly different business attitudes

CHAPTER ONE

TYPE OF COMMERCE	GOD	BUSINESS GOAL	ASSOCIATED WORLD VIEW
Trade	Urbanus	Final Sale Full Markup	Occam's Sledgehammer Practicality Sacred Numbers Rewardism Shopkeeperism
Industry	Ganesh	Lower Costs	Physical Resource Optimization Market Share Organizationalism Time-Based Efficiency People Resource Optimization
Clientry	Honestas	Lifelong Relations	Openness

among different cultures. The book examines specific attitudes toward work, friends, and ethics. These attitudes are part of the structure of thought and perception that we call culture. Clearly, some cultures are more adept at some functions than others. Within cultures, individual competencies vary as well.

The three gods of commerce in this book symbolize the three categories of commerce: trade, industry, and clientry. Each god is a metaphor for a world view or a cluster of world views that summarize the values, attitudes, perceptions, and behavior of a group of people.

CHAPTER TWO

URBANUS THE GOD OF TRADE

THE GOD OF TRADE IS AN URBAN GOD OF DIVERSITY, TOLERANCE, AND CONVIVIALITY.

Trade is an ancient human activity, and the proclivity for it is millennia old. There are differences of real significance in the details of trade—as is seen in the negotiations of a Lebanese Arab in Washington, D.C., versus the negotiations of a Chinese street vendor in Kowloon—but traders from different cultures have similar world views.

Cities are the by-product, nexus, and soul of trade. They are nearly always at the intersection of trade routes (unless they are deliberately anti-trade cities, like Brasilia). Once established, they become a driving force in trade, like Venice, Byzantium, London, Amsterdam, Hong Kong, and Singapore. Cities usually grew up around market sites because they offered long-term security for the storage of trade goods and security for the traders and craftspeople who made many of the goods. Rural and nomadic traders, by contrast, can support trade only at modest barter levels.

The god Urbanus is a god of diversity, tolerance, and conviviality. The word *urbane,* from the Latin word *urbanus,* for "city," has in fact come to mean "notably polite or finished in manner." Cities are not tied to agricultural seasons or the seasonal pasturing needs of animals. Cities run year-round, and their trade attracts a variety of people from other cities who introduce novel ideas and behaviors. The need for coexistence among these different peoples creates a climate of tolerance. Diversity in ethnicity, language, ideas, and behavior is necessary for the extension of trade and allows for the establishment of social institutions of tolerance. These institutions of tolerance are based on the business world view of practicality, a way of looking at the world that is uncomfortable with ideology and the concept of absolute truth.

Trade has a hub and spoke structure. At a hub site, trade goods are manufactured and sold and services are perfected. At sites at the ends of the spokes, goods are only sold.

Conviviality is endemic to trade, for the interaction of people at a hub site is vital. Conviviality is simply comfortable interaction, which is what great urban centers provide. A trader from Damascus can meet a trader from Timbuktu, for example, and the two can be comfortable enough to share information, exchange supplies, and possibly form a partnership.

Trade at sites at the ends of spokes by contrast, is prone to strain, anxiety, and distress due to the isolation of the trading partners. The kind of trade that takes place here is essentially the sale of the inventory, if it survives pirates and brigands.

Conviviality is a stable long-term state that promotes and supports trade at the hub. Where conviviality flourishes, trade flourishes. It is no accident that the great West African markets are relaxed, lively places with circuses and that the magnificent commercial city of Copenhagen has the Tivoli Gardens, a circus, in its downtown center. Most of the great commercial centers of the past were denounced by religious zealots as "sin cities" and "dens of iniquity" because they were areas of tolerance and conviviality.

The diversity, tolerance, and conviviality of the great urban commercial cities are necessary for trade. On the other hand, cities based on military, academic, or religious activity are rarely centers of successful commerce. Cities such as Annapolis, Maryland; Oxford. England; Jerusalem; and Mecca, for example, are weak in commerce.

Trade was flourishing in the middle-east a thousand years before the Old Testament was written. In Ebla, a Syrian trade town more than four thousand years old, archeologists have found ten thousand clay tablets containing bookkeeping information. The city carried on trade with Gaza, Jaffa, Damascus, Sodom, and Gomorrah. The biblical neighbors of the Hebrews were the Canaanites, who were probably the Phoenicians and who carried on trade throughout the Mediterranean.

Defining Trade

I've been in parts of central Africa where I could buy cassette tapes, but where there were no government nor business institutions, only traditional villages in a political no-man's land. While tape-recording machines were available, there was no electricity and no way to repair equipment. The machines were battery-operated, using tape cassettes and batteries from Japan, twelve thousand miles away.

Like these cassette tapes, batteries, and tape players, trade goods are found throughout the world. Trade is a basic human activity: Even in prisons, and in the most barren, desolate areas of the Arctic tundra, trade goes on.

Trade has several essential ingredients. They include markups, price competition, and credit.

I followed those tape players from central Africa along the trade route to the Congo. Each trader along the route marked the players up enough so that they could stay in business. The marked-up price included fresh replacement supplies, payment for the time involved in delivery and sale, additional related expenses such as storage and insurance, and a margin of profit to cover the uncertainty of staying in business.

Price competition is what the whole pipeline of trade goods is all about. The lowest-price final seller wins if he is paid his markup. If no one else is there to sell and no one is expected, the seller won't offer a low price.

Credit was extended in proportion to the stability of the situation. In an established market in Fez, Morocco, where the trader had operated a stall for generations, credit was extensive. In a Cameroon open market near a bus terminal, there was no credit. The cost of extending credit was simply added on to the price. An eight-dollar item, tape, was sold on credit for $10, with the first payment of cash at the time of sale being $6 and the second payment, weeks later, $4 if the seller had a better than 50 percent certainty of being paid the second installment.

The Five Business World Views of the Trader

Five business world views are worshiped in the house of Urbanus. These views are reflected in the pertinent questions most traders ask themselves: What's really going on here? (What's the deal on the table?) What is the evidence? (What is the product or service?) What are the numbers? What are the rewards? What changes will this transaction cause?

The trader has a world view that is quite different from that of the soldier, priest, bureaucrat, or employee. The trader knows the retail prices of many products and finds a source for those products at a low enough price to mark them up and sell them with sufficient margin to cover costs and to yield a profit.

Today, one world view of the trader (What are the numbers?) is reflected in American popular culture. Television shows like "The Price is Right" and "Name That Price" reward individuals who know the retail prices of certain items. The widespread presence of this world view is found today only in major industrial countries like the United States.

CHAPTER TWO
URBANUS

TYPE OF COMMERCE	GOD	BUSINESS GOAL	ASSOCIATED WORLD VIEW
Trade	Urbanus	Final Sale Full Markup	Occam's Sledgehammer Practicality Sacred Numbers Rewardism Shopkeeperism

What Is Really Going On: Occam's Sledgehammer

"Occam's razor," the thirteenth-century principle of analytical economy, holds that a simple explanation is better than an elaborate one. It is named for William of Occum, an empirically inclined philosopher at Oxford University who strongly opposed the elaborate medieval theologies of his time. His analysis was a "razor" because it sliced off all superfluous arguments. Occam's sledgehammer then, by extension, refers to an analysis that is not so delicate and precise in simplification, but crude and blunt in smashing away extraneous arguments.

Business people of all kinds (traders, industrialists, and clientrists) have this basic world view. A group of businesspeople listening to a lecture has several commonalties, one of which is that they are trying to discern the underlying message of the lecture. They are not enthralled by eloquent argument. Their mental question is "What is really being said here?" "Cut to the money. Cut to the chase."

Simple is not a philosophic concept to a businessperson. Instead, his or her notion of *simple* is rudimentary. To such a person, the meaning of *simple* is "nonnegotiability".

Academics, bureaucrats, and artists, on the other hand, have world views that are negotiable. The academic's world view is influenced by dialogue, fact, and knowledge. The bureaucrat's is negotiable under law and is influenced by both power and reason. The artist's world view is negotiable in response to vision, emotion, and talent. The business world view is a nonnegotiable domain. Everything in that world is built on some nonnegotiable structure.

The trader's world view has a very solid and very simple basis that is nonnegotiable in most circumstances, although it may not seem so on the surface.

A common image of trading is two traders in a tent over Turkish coffee, engaged in interminable negotiations over price. This activity only *seems* to be negotiation, however.

In reality, the two coffee-drinking traders are playing a skillful game with each other. Each has based his strategy on the knowledge of a nonnegotiable, unstated minimum sale price or maximum purchase price. The hospitality, bargaining, flattery, and courtesy of the setting all rest on the bedrock of the two nonnegotiable monetary sums. Unless both parties are satisfied by the terms of the deal, no transaction will take place.

Another common image of negotiating is that of a Japanese businessman, for example, offering a gift to the god of fortune, or an African trader offering a sacrifice to a local deity. In such a case, what looks like a negotiation with a deity is really the offer of a commission or a bribe instead. Both men believe that the deity can be swayed by such an offer. They are saying, "Please help me in my business, for I am worthy and pious," but as traders, what they are really saying is, "If you help me, I will be a loyal follower and a generous donor to your shrines and priests."

The nonnegotiable world view of a businessperson is very similar to that of a civil engineer's. Engineering designs are built on practical information, structural measurements, and mathematical formulas. Civil engineers are confident people with a black and white view of most elements of engineering. When a bridge is built to their specifications, they are confident that it will carry the intended load and not fall down.

Unlike the world view of the engineer, however, the nonnegotiable business world view allows for ambiguity about the future. The engineer may be certain he or she can build an enduring bridge, but the businessperson knows with similar certainty that local politics can stop the bridge from being built halfway through, close it once it's completed, and deny it maintenance funds in the future.

Imagine a businessperson being offered a free month's rent for signing a lease quickly without a final rereading of the contract. Very few would do so, not out of fear of manipulation or paranoia, but because the details of a lease agreement are often the foundation of business stability. A final contract is nonnegotiable; it is not to be trifled with even by accident or carelessness. Any proposed changes to a final contract will involve having a new contract drawn up.

Most world views are not like the businessperson's nonnegotiable way of seeing life. Instead, they are based on emotion, romanticism, and/or magic thinking. Nonnegotiability is perhaps the major distinguishing characteristic of the businessperson.

Show Me the Product/Service: Practicality

The business world view of practicality may sound like Jeremy Bentham's utilitarianism, or pragmatism, and it is indeed close. Bentham, an Oxford professor at the time of the American Revolution, argued for a fundamental social value: the greatest good for the greatest number, where good was based on a moral arithmetic weighing pleasure and pain. But practicality is simpler and more resilient than utilitarianism because it is a calculation of benefit from existing local available options.

A trader's world view is much closer to the empiricism of a technologist, like the inventor of the light bulb, Thomas Edison, who was also a businessman.

In the technical tradition, Edison was anti-theory. In developing the electric light bulb, he tried every kind of filament in order to find a suitable one. He carefully kept measurements of the durability and conductivity of each filament tested. This kind of empiricism almost defines technical development. Yet the inventor's world view is not precisely the business world view. The business world view includes more. Because it applies to the world of humans, it includes the reactions of other people who are themselves complex and unknowable domains.

Imagine a businessperson being offered a free month's rent on a lease if a neighboring tenant with a loud musical instrument (sounding most unpleasant to the businessperson) is permitted to continue occupying the adjacent rental space. In most cases, the businessperson would contact the tenant and attempt to negotiate a separate noise reduction agreement that would make the free month worthwhile. Businesspeople always try to find ways to make their world work better, financially and every other way.

Sacred Numbers

The business world view sees numbers as sacred and financial statements as divine. No good businessperson, and only a few mediocre ones, will do business without an understanding of balance sheets, income-expense statements, and cost data in dollars and units (of products and clients).

Business decisions are not based solely on measurement, many elements are factored in, but numbers are always the first consideration. Yes, in some instances there can be too many numbers. In the business world, however, having too many numbers is like having too much food: It may be a nuisance, but it is not a serious problem. Having too few numbers is like having too little food: It can be unpleasant and possibly fatal.

Engineers and inventors, of course, rely heavily on numbers. Numbers have a pervasiveness in the business world view that is even greater than in the world views of engineering and inventing. The businessperson doesn't just use numbers once in a while; rather he or she almost lives by numbers. Numbers are not just used to create a business, they are used to keep the business alive.

Imagine a businessperson offered a free month's rent on a lease with an offset of a 4 percent increase in the monthly rental for the first year, that is, one month free in exchange for eleven months at 4 percent more. Most businesspeople would redo their calculations carefully before accepting this offer. Rather than accept what seems to be an overall numeric advantage, most businesspeople would make sure that other incidental costs would not be increased because of the free month on the lease, realizing that the real net cost calculation might not be as favorable as the offer suggests.

For the businessperson, numbers govern not just the present but every eventuality of the future.

Rewardism

Rewardism is the belief that tangible rewards work. It is not the view that rewards *should* work, or that rewards are just, or that punishment is what works, only that rewards work. As Pavlov proved in regard to dogs and as B. F. Skinner proved in regard to humans, rewards can be used to change behavior.

There are many other systems besides rewardism. The Catholic Church has shaped human behavior for centuries with the minor promise of an afterlife but the major threat of eternal torment. Communism influenced behavior with promises of justice and an ideal society. The military is based on the concept of camaraderie and the severe threat of punishment.

Money is an excellent reward mechanism because it allows for the accumulation of rewards and the self-selection of rewards by the recipients. Multiple benefits are a part of any good reward system.

Imagine a businessperson being offered a free month's rent on a lease with some conditions attached. Most businesspeople would respond positively to such an offer because they understand the businesslike tactic of using rewards. However, they would also examine the offer carefully, because most would project onto the lessor a self-serving motive in offering a reward.

Shopkeeperism

One of the classic symbols of trade is the stereotypical French shopkeeper, who is opposed to any change whatsoever unless it reduces his or her taxes. Like this stereotype, many tradespeople are intensely conservative by nature. They hate change on principle. This attitude is often perceived as selfishness and greed, and although these emotions may be involved, the tradesperson hates change because of his or her desire for stability.

Stability, economic, legal, social, and physical, is what permits a tradesperson to plan and allows a business to thrive over time. Numbers to the businessperson are like sunlight to the desert farmer: ubiquitous. But just as fresh water is scarce for the farmer, so stability is scarce to the businessperson. Fresh water will produce plants in nearly dry soil, turning a desert into a luxuriant oasis. Stability creates a vibrant, thriving commercial community. Therefore, a stable social system is like a well-maintained irrigation system.

Traders can operate anywhere. Although their price markup rises as social instability increases, trade is more likely to flourish over time in a stable environment. Traders want stability, and stability is conservative.

Trading operates without theories, and often even without good ideas. It is inherently conservative because it only knows what works, or what customers are buying now. Any change is more likely to lead to a loss of customers and revenue than to an increase, so conservatism is mandatory. Changes in the operation and marketing of a business need to be glacially slow for empirical reasons, and they need careful measurement to determine their impact on customer behavior.

The confusing thing about the shopkeeper business world view is that business people are frequently the cause of much of the change they abhor. For example, in a suburb of Portland, Maine, the local Chamber of Commerce was up in arms because a large supermarket was moving into a small town and displacing local small businesses. On a national level the Chamber of Commerce has made notable statements about declining moral values as fewer women stay home to care for children. Yet their own members are the business people who are opening the larger supermarkets and hiring women into the labor force.

It is not hard to identify the problems trade creates. Picture the national Chamber of Commerce lobbying against the expansion of national health care because it will drive up taxes for its members. At the same time, a small group of the Chamber's members comes to see their national lobbyists to oppose the organization's lobbying because this small group has been profiting greatly from the rapid introduction of new medical technologies. The very technologies that are making medical costs higher thus create political pressure for a national health care program.

Summary

Trade is the most ancient form of business. Urbanus is its god because trade originated in urban areas that provided a crossroads where different kinds of people could exchange goods, services, and information. Urban areas are the convivial hub, while the ends of the spokes are the hinterland where goods are sold in small numbers of units. Trade is based on making the final sale and getting the right markup on goods and services sold; it also involves price competition and sometimes credit.

Traders (and businesspeople whose views are built on those of traders) have five basic ways of looking at the world:

1. They want everything simplified so they know the basic, non-negotiable facts.
2. They will use every variable they can find to make business work.
3. Their world is governed by numbers: money and units of goods.
4. They believe most people's behavior can be influenced through positive tangible rewards.
5. The trader knows for sure only what is currently working, and therefore resists change.

The Language of Urbanus

The language of Urbanus is money. Commerce came before money, of course, when farmers and nomads traded by bartering. But money allows commerce to flourish.

But what is money? It is the form of communication used throughout the domain of commerce. It is unique to commerce and is not the medium of communication in theology, the military, dance, or pedagogy.

There is an American adage that "money talks." Meaning if you have money you get your way, and that people pay attention to someone with money. This adage recognizes that money is language. At the same time, it implies that a direct connection exists between money and power. It does not. It is sometimes true because many people want money and will respond to incentives of the people offering money. However, it is not universally true. Some rich people are pathetically powerless, while some very powerful people have little money. Heirs and heiress are frequently the victims of scams, con artists, and social climbing predators who gain complete control over them. Some public figures, such as Dwight Eisenhower and Martin Luther King Jr were powerful, but not rich.

Money as Language

Some writers have observed that money has several of the same qualities as language: It is pervasive among humans and it takes many forms (checks, bonds, cigarettes in prison, etc.), it is symbolic, and is a tool of communication. It is true that wherever there is commerce, there is money, with the exception of silent trade. This occurs in the rare cases in which two neighboring tribes are mutually hostile but are willing to trade. This has been reported in a half dozen cases around the world. Each tribe displays their offering on opposite sides of a riverbank. When the goods on each side are considered equal, the exchange occurs. The exception proves the rule in this case, however, because it is obvious how much easier the whole transaction would be with money.

Language is not a metaphor for money, nor is money *like* language; instead, it *is* a language. Money is the language of commerce. American money is a specific kind of monetary language, just as English is a specific kind of verbal language.

The Encyclopedia Britannica defines *language* as "arbitrary vocal symbols by means of which social groups cooperate." Language is thus a symbolic system of communication used by both humans and animals. It is common knowledge that whales and birds pick up variations on their songs while associating with other whales and birds.

Such songs are a kind of language, like the dance a bee does to direct the other bees to nectar. When bees are taken to new environments, they adapt their dance accordingly. These dances are symbolic movements with broad contextual meanings.

The dance of the bees is like the signing that is used by the deaf. (Interestingly, sign language is different for each linguistic culture. There is an American sign language and a Greek sign language. Because sign language uses the hands instead of the vocal cords, it is different syntactically from spoken language. Sign language among experienced users is not as linear as spoken language.)

Other systems of communication that can be considered languages are facial expressions and mathematics. Language involves interaction between people and usually some behavioral consequences of that interaction.

Other activities that can be considered forms of language include music, dance, and fine art, all of which can convey meaning and emotion.

Symbols and Context

Money is purely symbolic. It is definitely not good as food or fertilizer. It rarely functions as a sun shade, a tool, or a weapon, and is not good for starting fires. It is a symbol. Symbols have distinct meaning only in context.

Context is determinate when it comes to symbols. A piece of colored cloth can be a national flag or a diaper, depending on the context. In the context of an emergency, it can be both.

Generally, money is a form of commercial encouragement, an inducement toward a desired behavior. If you buy something from me several times, I'll probably try to keep on having that item available for you.

This encouragement occurs on a large and small scale: Buying crude oil from the Saudis or gasoline from a neighborhood station are both commercial encouragement.

Symbolic commercial encouragement can come in innumerable different forms, such as wages, purchase price, or even tips.

Money is also used to discourage, as in cutting an employee's pay or bonus in order to get rid of him or her.

Symbols gain their meaning in context. The same symbol does not always retain the same meaning. The act of offering one dollar in payment for a cup of coffee can be an insult, a charming act, or a joke.

It's an insult if you pay your host in his own house after he serves you breakfast. It's an act of charm if you are a grandfather and the dollar is gift-wrapped for your six-year-old grandchild. It's a joke when the boss brings coffee to the secretary and she hands him a dollar. The commercial context of the language of money is the transaction.

Just as a verbal language is made up of many words, money comes in a wide variety of forms. Bus tokens, credit cards, equity securities, invoices, letters of credit, and dozens of debenture forms are all forms of money. Near-cash forms range from bankers' acceptances and repos to certificates of deposit. Just as a verbal language changes, dropping old words and adopting new ones, old forms of money fall out of favor as new ones are generated. Uses also change, as is the case of the functional role of stocks and bonds reversing itself in the past sixty years. In the 1920s stocks were slow moving and bonds were volatile. New forms of money are borrowed from other cultures; witness the fairly recent "bankable corporate payable" from Japan.

Rules of Commercial Grammar

Money, like grammar, has rules. The following are some examples of such rules.

Money has forms that are acceptable and unacceptable. Illegal activities such as prostitution, numbers runners, and dope dealers want cash in advance. Moreover, the cash must be in bills under $200, because banks are required to register denominations of $200 and over. McDonald's, the Bremerton Ferry and many parking garages want cash. Car rental companies only want credit cards. Hospital emergency rooms want credit cards or proof of insurance coverage. Try to pay cash to delivery room doctors and nurses when a baby is born and you'll create pandemonium.

There are times and places where the offer of money is unacceptable. Consider openly carrying on business at a funeral or offering money to a lover during private sex. Consider a courtroom defendant making pecuniary offers to a judge or jury.

Money agreements are social as well as legal contracts. The person who doesn't pay personal debts on time or bounces checks, may evoke adverse social responses, such as exclusion from parties or private clubs. They may also have trouble renting apartments or getting job promotions.

Money agreements can be manipulated to convey information. If you are dissatisfied with the work of an interior designer, taking six months to pay the bill conveys your attitude.

Because money is a language, different commercial cultures follow different monetary rules. In Japan, wedding guests are given money in an envelope rather than the guests giving wedding gifts. Japanese children do not receive allowances. In a Syrian street market, the member of one family might pay five hundred dollars for a horse that elicits a payment of eight hundred dollars from another family. (Social status influences selling prices.) In the United States, wealthy people can expect less-wealthy social climbers to pick up the tab for a meal. In Mexico or Ghana, this would never happen. In Japan and Sweden, a taxi driver will return a tip. In New York, you may be verbally assaulted for not giving the driver a sufficiently large tip. Only in the United States and Canada can you pay for merchandise and service with a bank check, then stop payment on the check. While stopping payment rarely occurs in the United States, accepting checks for merchandise or service itself is rare in other parts of the world.

Money is the extremely effective and flexible language of commerce. The American monetary system of dollars and cents is our commercial language.

CHAPTER THREE

GANESH THE GOD OF INDUSTRY

GANESH, THE INDIAN GOD OF IMPROVEMENT, IS THE GOD OF INDUSTRY.

When the core locations that generated trade became sufficiently large and stable, other institutions, such as banking, corporations, insurance, and international contract law, were developed. This was the beginnings of industry. Industry is different from trade. Unlike trade, industry focuses on the reduction of costs and adds four additional elements to the world view of its successful practioners.

The god of industry is Ganesh, an elephant-headed deity usually portrayed astride a mouse. With four arms and a broken tusk, often painted red, Ganesh is the remover of obstacles. When an Indian starts a new venture, he or she invokes the good will of Ganesh, who symbolizes the belief that difficulties can be overcome.

I once visited a school in Lucknow, India, where very unlikely people (retired military) were being instructed in entrepreneurship. The dean explained that the most important lesson the school had to teach was the possibility of improvement. The possibility of improvement is based on the idea that something better than that which exists at present is both achievable and desirable. Improvement in this sense parallels the American notion of progress.

The founder of modern India was Bal Gangadhar Tilak, a philosopher who began the movement for independence from Britain in the nineteenth century. Tilak chose Ganesh from a panoply of Indian gods to be the symbol of the future nation, and reinstituted local celebrations of Ganesh throughout India. His choice of the symbol was astute. India continues to make large strides in becoming an important industrial country. India had been a traditional society where most people accepted the world the way it was and assumed that nothing had changed in the past nor should change in the future.

CHAPTER THREE
GANESH

TYPE OF COMMERCE	GOD	BUSINESS GOAL	ASSOCIATED WORLD VIEW
Industry	Ganesh	Lower Costs	Physical Resource Optimization
			Market Share
			Organizationalism
			Time-Based Efficiency
			People Resource Optimization

The willingness to make changes and a belief in the possibility of improvement are not widely held qualities in the world. In fact, these characteristics seem to distinguish industrial societies from traditional societies. Resistance comes from a number of sources. There's the popular view that the old ways are always superior to the new. There is also the view that family structure and tradition are sacred and will suffer from any change. The presence of traders selling their goods, does not appear to disrupt traditional societies because trade doesn't rest on a notion of improvement. Instead, it is based on the status quo and on maintaining stability.

The willingness of a people and a society to improve is the necessary fertile soil that industry needs in order to grow. Industry does change traditional society, in many cases, eliminating it.

What Is Industry?

As we have discussed, trade is pervasive. Industry, on the other hand, is limited to a small number of originating nations. Trade focuses on the single final sale at the highest price the seller can extract; industry aims at economies of scale and market share, with the goal of growing sales volume.

Industry is an outgrowth of dense trade and is based on large markets and reducing costs. The real genius of John D. Rockefeller was that he found a way to produce kerosene at a quarter of the cost of all the other wildcatters in the kerosene industry. At the time, a barrel of crude oil could be refined to kerosene at $2.00 per barrel. Rockefeller found he could do it for under $1.00 when doing hundreds of barrels and for under $.50 when doing thousands of barrels. He then had to create a large market to take advantage of his much greater profit margin at high levels of production (economies of scale).

Like other giant businesses of the industrial world (steel and chemicals), the technology of cost reduction associated with economies of scale forced industrialists to find large and growing markets. The steam revolution and the railroad revolution allowed industrialists to cut costs significantly, which became an advantage only when large markets were developed for buying.

A large market is the byproduct of political and social stability. That's why the United States has become such an important industrial society. The colonial English, French, and Dutch systems also provided a stable economic and political system that allowed for mass distribution, which in turn took advantage of technologies that created further economies of scale.

The objective of economies of scale is to keep reducing the cost of production, so that the low final prices create monopolistic conditions that deter other entrants to the industry. Having found a way to reduce costs, it's important to keep doing so at higher and higher levels of production to keep competitors out of an industry by effectively undercutting their prices. This is the classical economic analysis of industrial society. Karl Marx was fairly accurate in his analysis of these elements, 130 years ago.

Thanks to the Japanese, economists recently have learned that the new objective of industry is to gain market share. The Japanese found that by obtaining a significant stable market share, especially with brand names like Sony, Panasonic, Bridgestone, and Honda, the industrial company could introduce new products and achieve widespread acceptance that would allow them to scale up the production of new goods to the levels where economy of scale was highly profitable. Sony was a trusted brand with good market share in the late 1970s. It introduced an innovative new product, the Sony Walkman, and within one year was producing over one million Walkmans. Prior to the Japanese model, companies created new markets for each new product.

The Role of Government

To get a larger market in the first place, it is usually necessary to utilize government. Government can provide market stability. It creates homogeneity and suppresses rebellion and anarchy, both conditions unfavorable to industry. It is to government that we owe the standard time zones that make it efficient to run railroads; eminent domain and free land for railroads; dams and water systems; sewer systems; electric lighting; roads and highways; canals; and courts to enforce contracts to make bond and equity markets possible. The list is long. In Russia and China, governments did not provide these services to benefit business, and thus their industrial systems are underdeveloped compared to those in the United States.

Political and social stability foster larger markets. Democratic governments happen to be especially useful in creating political and social stability. They are also fairly easy for industry to influence. Industry needs government, and it needs government that is responsive to its concerns. That is precisely what was absent in the Soviet Union for seventy years, in China for forty years, and in India for thirty years.

Many people assume that government and business interests are in conflict, because corporate lobbyists complain so incessantly about regulation and taxes. But the opposite is true: Business desperately needs government, a point well established by the economist Mancur Olson in *The Rise and Decline of Nations* and several other respected books.

It is desirable that industry be able to influence government. Business needs to have property protected. It needs stability. It needs incomes to be as stable as possible. It needs workers to be educated. It needs a prosperous middle class. It needs a wide range of services and systems.

Many industrialists and some of their lobbying organizations still think like traders and don't fully appreciate the industrial needs for government.

The Four Business World Views Associated with Industrialism

Physical Resource Optimization

Physical resource optimization means viewing all the physical objects in the world as susceptible to change or modification in order to benefit business. It means building the steel plant near the coal and iron ore sources, then building a rail line to the closest distribution center. It means locating a mail-order warehouse at the airport.

The industrialist looks at all physical resources as having a price or a cost as inputs to the business or in distribution. The industrialist then considers the multiple ways these resources can be reorganized to reduce the costs of production.

This world view is quite different from that of the trader, out in rural areas selling trade goods, who usually has a traditional view of the world and accepts life the way it is.

We Americans have become fairly comfortable with this physical resource optimization business world view; in fact we usually have it ourselves. We will remove trees on our property for a roadway, will level the top of a hill for a house, will dig a long trench for pipes or wires. Our railroads are usually built in straight lines, which means leveling hills and carving mountains. Traditional societies reject this view of the physical world. Thus, Native Americans have strongly resisted railroads, mining sites, and timber projects that threatened to violated sacred lands. A traditional footpath, which can still be found in many places, (I know of several in national parks near my home) meanders — around rocks and trees, even around trees that no longer exist.

This world view has led industry into such popular activities as steadily reducing commodity prices over the past one hundred years, improving the quality of goods, and developing goods and services that make life more convenient for the consumer. This same world view, though, leads to such unpopular actions as disrupting natural systems by clear-cutting forests, filling in marshes, building highways, and starting wars to acquire or to protect supplies.

To better understand this business world view, imagine a businessperson being offered a free month's rent on a lease if the owner of the building space is allowed to move the loading dock one hundred yards farther away from the main operating activities. The industrialist will calculate the value of one month's rent versus the added transportation costs and the added labor costs over the length of the lease. The decision to accept the offer will be made based on the physical advantages of the rental space to the industrialist.

Organizationalism

The second industrialist world view is that of seeing the world in terms of organizations. The word *organization* is used broadly by anthropologists to include tribal groupings, and kinship groupings. The industrialist is more likely to define *organization* as a group of people acting from common financial interests. Such organizations, of course, play a large role in business life.

Industries generally prefer larger organizations to smaller ones. Companies will usually choose a large supplier with a long history of good quality over many smaller suppliers. They will buy out a supplier if they believe they can manage that aspect of the business better. Size is not the only determinant, however. A company may choose to work with another company as a supplier when religious or school friendship bonds exist, because such bonds create reliability and trust.

The Advantages of Organization

The industrialist sees the world in terms of organization because her or she is interested in acting in the world with dispatch and alacrity. Doing so requires understanding the group connections among people that influence them such as their church, alumni group, sorority, or professional association. When there is a business interest in larger market share or strong customer loyalty, there is a need to see customers in terms of their clustering behavior.

The educational and economic demographics of consumers are important to automobile producers. Sports affinities among consumers are important to beer producers. Professional identities are relevant to convention businesses. Enduring relationships with one's alumni association, political party, and occupational cohort lead to organizational consequences of relevance to various businesses.

Most non-businesspeople, probably four out of five, rarely or never think in organizational terms. When a non-industrialist wants to buy a car, he or she asks friends, checks ads, and shops around. One who thinks like an industrialist would be more likely to ask the organizations he or she belongs to, such as a credit union, if they have automobile purchasing affiliations. Such a person might ask whether their country club might be making a group car purchase for its members, or whether a friend knows of some special institutional situation where cars are being handled differently from the way they are in standard retail outlets.

Time-Based Efficiency

The conservation and allocation of time as a scarce resource is the central tenet of efficiency. It should not be surprising, then, that supplicants in the church of Ganesh wear miniature clocks on our wrists.

Clocks are intimately associated with the development of industry. A superb historical study of this subject is *Revolution in Time,* by David S. Landes. As he points out, wooden town clocks began to appear in seventeenth-century Europe as an outgrowth of monastic manufacturing and the needs of trade. By the eighteenth century, such clocks were made from metal and house clocks had become the prized possessions of the trader class.

Traders were beginning to conserve time. Time precision came to be counted in minutes, so that traders could schedule their mutual business meetings effectively. With the rise of factories in the early nineteenth century, public clocks and the punch-in time clock became key elements in the development of wage labor. Later in the century, chronometers made ocean exploration more exact and watches made trains safer and more reliable.

Watches have become almost ubiquitous on the planet, but this should not mislead the reader about their central industrial role. Most watches I've seen in the rural areas of developing countries are strictly ornamental; meetings scheduled for 2 p.m. occur within two hours of 2 p.m. at best. Agricultural people have gods of the seasons, but not of time in the industrial sense.

The elevation of time to a central human concern has been very slow to develop. Where it *has* developed in Asia, it has developed somewhat differently than in Europe. According to Charles Hampden-Turner in *The Seven Cultures of Capitalism,* the world view of time-based efficiency has at least two major divisions: linear and synchronous. In European parts of the world, planning is linear and parallel. Segments are completed as a sub-assembly to be brought together into a sequential and larger assembly. In many parts of industrial Asia, on the other hand, simultaneous parts interact as the assembly proceeds, and congruence, rather than parallelism, is apparent.

We are all familiar with the concept of efficiency on a personal scale. We know that if the subway is faster and cheaper to ride than the bus, the subway is more efficient. Modern Americans have so readily internalized this value that we hardly recognize it as a world view. We know how to weigh several options, calculate their convenience and expense, and find the most efficient.

When arguments are made against one form of efficiency, they are often based in finding more efficiency at a higher level. For example, the subway may be more efficient than a bus to the individual passenger. To a city manager, however, a bus system may be preferable to the subway because it is a more flexible mode for urban society: Over decades, bus routes can be changed very quickly but subway routes can't. In this case an appeal to time efficiency occurs at a higher order of calculation.

When efficiency is a world view, it has a surprising consequence: It can be anti-traditional and anti-status quo. Because the business world view of the industrialist includes time efficiency, it is distinctly different from the trader's bourgeois view.

The assembly line, a major innovation using time-based efficiency, resulted in low-cost cars and a radically changed America. In the past generation in America, some retailers have made a better time use of their facilities by staying open longer and more often—as many as twenty-four hours a day and seven days a week—creating a world of nighttime social denizens and virtually eliminating Sunday sabbath traditions.

People Resource Optimization

In the business world view, people can be subjected to the same criterion of efficiency as other physical resources. This view was first manifested in the hiring and firing of blue collar workers at the whim of industrialists. Today, almost all employees are subject to this view. Since this world view was originally focused only on unskilled and low-wage workers, it came as a surprise when it was also applied to skilled and professional employees. But the logic is the same.

People resource optimization has both benefits and shortcomings. The cold rationality of viewing people as physical resources demolished older business stereotypes about gender and brought women into the workplace in the United States in the early 1960s. That in turn made divorce and single parenthood a more viable personal choice for women. The same view is behind the movement of factories to Mexico and Asia.

In some cultures, this industrial world view is not fully developed, which has noticeably affected the market. In both the Chinese and Latin cultures, the concept of family is so central that in business close family members cannot be treated like regular employees or partners. Consequently, corporate founders tend to pass on their businesses to family members instead of to professional managers. Family members seldom have the skills of a founder, however, and private industries established by native Chinese and Latin Americans rarely grow large and almost never survive several generations.

Summary

Ganesh is the god of industry, because he symbolizes the possibility of improvement. Industry is founded on the principle of improvement.

Unlike trade, industrialism does not thrive everywhere in human culture. Nor does it aim for a markup on each final sale, but instead focuses on reducing costs.

Cost reduction requires large markets and a high volume of final sales. Large markets require economic stability. Government is necessary to provide economic stability for large markets; therefore, industry needs sympathetic government.

The trader can buy and sell products in a world with little or no government and without disrupting traditional society. Industry, by contrast, needs a stable social and economic environment and develops only within the context of a well-governed state.

The four world views of the industrialist significantly change the status quo because they involve altering the physical world, forming new organizational systems, managing time, and seeing people as physical resources.

Social Sorting:
Understanding Organizations

The organizational world view is so basic to industrialism that it is helpful to study that view in more detail. As we have discussed, the industrialist sees the world in terms of organizational systems. The key to understanding human organizations is the phenomenon of social sorting.

The growth of industrial society occurred in Europe at a time when the traditional society was breaking down. Industry contributed to this societal breakdown, weakening the three great powers: the church, the king, and the military. To replace these three entities, commercial society created new organizations: guilds, corporations, secret societies (Freemasons, the Knights of Columbus), and later, political parties, unions, and voluntary civic associations. Individuals moved from being rigidly controlled by the hierarchical dictates of the traditional society, to a level of autonomy appropriate to the new voluntary and commercial organizations.

The new industrial world of the 1800s introduced widespread social migration and personal independence. Individuals began to organize their lives according to personal needs, desires, and goals. The structure of society was thus slowly reorganized.

What Is the Nature of Commercial
and Voluntary Organizations?

Many consultants and business advisors who have worked with
a wide variety of businesses have been discouraged by the slow rate
of change they encounter. They mistakenly assume that only large
numbers of people are inherently resistant to change.

If they haven't had experience with small- to medium-sized
companies, they assume that large size is the problem. Small companies, however, are also resistant to change. The real problem is
much more fundamental, and applies to many organizations other
than businesses.

Non-changing Organizations

Why is it so hard to change the direction of a business or the
behavior of a government agency? Why has Berkeley, California,
always been so radical? Why are television evangelists so popular today?

These seemingly diverse phenomena are closely related, and
one explanation applies to all of them. Let's start with the question
of why it is so hard to change a business.

Changing a business in nearly any way, as most consultants and
managers will gladly attest, is extremely difficult. The reason is that a
"business" is a group of people who have come together as a result
of a very thorough sorting process. Each group of people we call a
business is made up of remarkably similar individuals, thanks to a
phenomenon called social sorting.

What Are the Main Components of Social Sorting?

Social sorting consists of three components: the flag, the screen, and the washout. These are the components when specifically applied to business:

1. The Flag is the information "lure" that draws the prospective employee to the business.
• An individual who lacks employment looks for a job.
• An individual is interested in a particular business because of something positive he or she has learned about that business.
• The individual applies for the job.
2. The Screen is the variety of tests applied to the applicant throughout the hiring phase (including interviews, job references and requirements, and the trial work period).
• The individual contacts the personnel department for preliminary screening, with a second screening by the appropriate department head and supervisor.
• The individual's credentials from previous jobs and schools are checked by the hiring company.
• The individual is hired on a probationary basis for day-to-day observation.
3. The Washout is the process of surviving the first few years as an employee of a business. Attrition occurs because people discover that they don't fit the standards—or that the standards don't fit them.
• The individual feels comfortable enough in the new business to remain for several years and decline other job offers.

Social Sorting

When fine sand is sifted through many screens, the final collection of particles reveals a grouping remarkably similar in size and shape. The same is true for the sorting process of employees.

In screening sand, only two dimensions are selected: mass and volume. The employee selection process involves screening by multiple dimensions over several years. The end result is a group of people who are more like each other than grains of sand could ever be. For like-minded people in a business to transform themselves of their own volition is thus highly unlikely.

This process of forming a group of people called "a business" is known as social sorting.

Where Else Is Social Sorting Found?

Social sorting helps to explain the tendency for political districts to vote the same way over decades and centuries, the concentration of high-tech businesses in few geographic areas, and the current power of Christian fundamentalism.

The range of phenomena considered examples of social sorting is vast. As well as businesses, it includes government agencies and voluntary organizations such as clubs and political parties. The particular differences among these three groups concern the relative significance and distinct mechanisms of their sorting elements. In other words, the three elements, **flag**, **screen** and **washout**, operate in different ways and in different degrees within these groups.

Government Jobs

In a government agency, the washout function is dramatically weaker than in a profit-making business. Government agency employees are protected by civil service laws. The flag that attracts the prospective government agency employee has a perceptibly different message ("Join us for a boring but secure life") from the "Come help us make money" message sent by a profitable business.

Voluntary Associations

Screening is negligible in a club such as the PTA or a political party. It's the washout factor that determines membership here; that is, those who stay are the ones who find the other members comfortable and rewarding to be with.

Political Districts

In political districts, the washouts are very gradual, occurring over long periods of time. Upstate and downstate New York have voted in opposite ways from the very first election in that state, which has always been characterized by "the Madison people" versus "the Hamilton people." Californians have split their tickets (different parties for adjacent public offices) since it was given statehood. Berkeley, California, is the same politically radical city today as it was half a century ago, when it elected its first radical mayor.

People who are born and grow up in a region that has different values than their own will move away when they are old enough to do so. People who move to a new area find a way to leave if they can't accommodate their attitudes to feel comfortable with their neighbors.

The Geographic Sorting Process

Americans move many times in their lives; 50 percent have moved in the past three years and 75 percent in the past five years. This kind of mobility creates a geographic sorting process.

Friends who have paid attention to their primary and secondary school alumni gatherings report that even in rural areas, less than one third of their fellow students have remained in the same region. The rest sorted themselves out to places that were a better fit. New residents to locales are usually attracted by the characteristics of the people who are already living there, continuing the sorting process.

Silicon Valley

Why did so many high-tech developers start their companies in Sunnyvale, California, creating the now world-famous Silicon Valley? The original entrepreneurs could have recruited lower-cost employees in any community within twenty miles of Sunnyvale. They also might have found prospective employees who were better educated in the liberal arts twenty-five miles away at U.C. Berkeley. But Silicon Valley's existing Sunnyvale community had exactly the right mix for the entrepreneurs. Electronic engineers and technical assemblyline workers were abundant among civilians working in military jobs. The community was presorted on key dimensions to become the future center of micro-electronics.

Television and the Modern Baptists

What is the cause of the recent popularity and resultant political power of television evangelists? Television Christian fundamentalists are a primary example of the effectiveness of the social-sorting flag.

There are twenty million Baptists in the United States, including fundamentalists and evangelicals. In turn, fundamentalists and evangelicals make up more than half of the total number of Baptists. This segment of society has remained the same relative size for over a century (new Mexican immigrants are the only growing part of the evangelicals), but has exerted very little political influence in the past, because they have not been organized into one large group. This is the case even in the South, where the concentration of Baptists is the greatest.

The most important Baptist church organization is the relatively autonomous individual church, which is led by a pastor. There are weak Baptist affiliate organizations. The individual churches of most other Protestant denominations are governed by larger organizations, such as the Presbyterian and Lutheran synods and the Methodist "conference," which designates ministers' church assignments.

Because of these strong umbrella organizations, Presbyterian, Lutheran, and Methodist religious groups have historically played much more powerful roles in national politics than the locally-isolated Baptist churches.

In recent years, television has allowed some Baptist churches, sorting their prospective members out from the rest with the flag of a particular religious ideology (a fourteen-point "doctrine"), to grow to very large sizes. One church with an ongoing television ministry can have over a million members. The television ministry is very effective when it comes to raising money and sending letters to Congress. The large numbers of participants involved in these church lobbying efforts were not possible when the flag was limited to one person (the pastor) in one church building.

Billy Graham did create a large Baptist church out of this same denominational grouping. Staging tent shows in city after city, Graham gained large numbers of followers through a relatively ambiguous theology. His theology was too ecumenical, however, to create a powerful political machine.

Social Sorting and Cults

How does a Reverend Jim Jones's People's Temple mass suicide happen? People's Temple was a washout phenomenon of a particular nature. Jones had a large, devoted organization along traditional church lines. Over time, he became progressively more paranoid, possibly because of drugs and medicine. As his managerial demands became increasingly unreasonable, his assistants objected and confronted him. Jones's opponents found that they could not form easy coalitions with other managerial supporters, partly because Jones personally rewarded his supporters.

A gradual washout occurred, with wiser opponents quitting as Jones's demands became more and more objectionable. The sycophantic managers who remained behind were the least qualified to halt Jones's madness. The organization proceeded to go berserk.

Will similar cult events happen in the future? As long as there are organizations headed by a single charismatic individual, the same phenomenon is likely to occur again and again.

How to Use Social Sorting

Social sorting is obviously an important analytic tool. How can it be used positively to benefit society?

Many governmental processes can be improved by understanding and employing social sorting. Appointed boards, panels, and commissions frequently are of inconsistent quality. By determining the desired attributes for the board, panel, or commission, and specifying processes that select people with these attributes, group composition can be changed dramatically over time.

For example, parole boards need specific attributes for handling difficult convicts. In addition, some mature compassion is desirable. The board might be designated by law to have a fixed membership consisting of a naval chief petty officer with five years' service in grade, a minister with fifteen years' active service in local churches and a high school gym instructor with ten years' experience. The net result will be a consistent quality of behavior in line with the designated goals of the parole board.

Merger Messes

The concept of social sorting could be used to good effect in studying possible corporate mergers. Mergers of small- and medium-sized companies sometimes make disastrous combinations. Very large companies necessarily have an employee base that is not significantly different from the population as a whole, and usually survive mergers. Smaller companies, with their highly-screened, individualized groups of employees, are more resistant to merging successfully with other companies of similar size. Merging

Princeton University and the Arizona College of Mines, for example, would not improve either organization, but corporate mergers of the same kind are attempted all the time.

Reforming Renegade Agencies

Reforming such specialized organizations as the FBI, DEA, ATF, or CIA would seem an almost hopeless task.

Say the goal is to curtail the increasingly erratic (and illegal) activity of one of these agencies. There is a solution but it is not to bring in a new top management. Top management can do nothing to change the existing sort of employees. If they bring in a new type of employee, the existing employees will make it too uncomfortable for new ones to stay.

The solution is to merge the renegade agency into a larger benign organization. Aggressive managers from the old renegade organization will then seek upward mobility into the larger, newer one, where they will have to cope with a new set of organizational goals. The older departments will thus lose vitality and accommodate to the new overall organizational standards.

Organizations: Complexity and Cohesion

Almost everyone understands the concept of organization. It is, of course, the principle behind team sports. Football teams, to take one instance, are highly structured organizations with individuals and groups performing highly specialized functions: offensive teams, defensive teams, kickers, halfbacks, and numerous types of coaches.

Organization is the invisible structure of the systems that surround our lives. In the past, we have often been led to believe that the invisible hand of the competitive market is responsible for the way our society functions. Behind market activities, however, is social organization.

Have you ever wondered why strangers on the beach tan themselves equidistant from each other? Or how eighty million turkeys get delivered three days before Thanksgiving, with very few left over? Or why, when the speed limit was reduced to 55 miles per hour in the late 1970s, traffic fatalities declined? All of these phenomena are the result of organizational structure operating in our lives.

Cohesion and Complexity

The chart on the next page summarizes the concept of organizational structure as a reflection of interpersonal cohesion and task-related complexity.

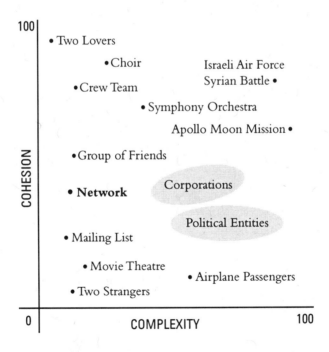

Cohesion

The left side of the chart measures interpersonal cohesion. The strongest cohesive group is two lovers, the weakest two strangers. Other examples of extremely cohesive groups are a choir and a crew team—these groups even breathe together.

A group that experiences dehesion, or strong hostility among the members, would be placed below the 0-degree mark on the cohesion rule. An example of this kind of group would be prisoners fighting among themselves.

Complexity

The bottom scale of the chart measures the task-related complexity of the groups listed. At the extreme right is the Apollo moon mission, the most complex human endeavor of recent times. Putting men on the moon involved the coordination of millions of people, from those who built rockets and rocket parts to the tens of millions whose taxes paid for the excursion. Errors of as little as .01 percent in the rockets and capsules would have kept the project from succeeding; most error tolerances were hundreds of times smaller. Organization was the key.

The group with the least organizational complexity is two strangers passing on the street. Neither education, communication, nor coordination is involved in this group.

Scattered across the chart are examples of diverse organizations. A symphony orchestra is in the upper middle, because it requires a great deal of training and must be cohesive to the fraction of a second. The amount of education, skill, experience, and support staff required to make a symphony work is very large.

Corporations are in the large ellipse in the middle. They require far less cohesiveness than a symphony, but in some cases, such as an airline or telephone company, they require careful coordination, training, and mutual support among tens of thousands of people, with a very low tolerance for error.

Low Complexity and Weak Cohesion

Strangers on the beach are examples of weak cohesion and low complexity. But observation shows us that people nearly always sit equidistant from each other, where terrain permits. They organize themselves just enough to communicate to everyone around them that they don't want to communicate unnecessarily. By tradition, in the United States communication becomes necessary only when one person needs help in an emergency or has forgotten to bring something to the beach that another might spare, such as water, suntan lotion, or catsup.

Moviegoers and airplane passengers are found on the lower end of the cohesion scale. In both instances, strangers are sitting in close proximity, so cohesion is low. However, the complexity of these two examples differs from that of two strangers passing in the street, because potential coordinated behavior is implicit at every moment. Moviegoer and plane passenger egress in case of a disaster has been previously planned and prepared for. Possible disasters have been anticipated, and emergency measures have been built into the training of flight attendants. All airlines carry medical supplies to be used by the medical personnel statistically likely to be among the passengers in case of a stroke or heart attack emergency. The complexity in this situation is comparable to but considerably higher than in a movie theatre. In both the theatre and the airplane, even the air supply is provided; in the airplane, it is a vital matter.

Political organizations, while weaker on the cohesion scale than commercial organizations, extend farther on the complexity scale. Political organizations rarely have as great a cohesive quality as the prototypical corporation, because political organizations (including most government agencies) have little or weak screening of their new members. Corporations tend to hire only people who are like their existing employees.

Political organizations often deal with far greater technical and social complexities than do commercial business. Government institutions must always satisfy a diverse group of constituencies and goals. The Peace Corps has employees, volunteers, Congress, host countries, the State Department, and intelligence agencies to deal with in addition to its stated goals and changing strategies. A commercial business has a narrower focus, with fairly clear and measurable goals such as growth and making a net profit.

Strong Cohesion, Low and High Complexity

Two interesting entries on this chart are the two lovers and the 1978 Israeli Air Force strike against Syria.

Two lovers have high cohesion and low complexity. As they get more involved by moving into the same living space and/or marrying and having children, the complexity increases. Usually this process is gradual, to allow the appropriate support structures of friends and family to develop around them.

The 1978 battle between Syria and the Israeli Air Force ranks as an event of extraordinary cohesion and complexity. A small group of men, working together with a level of precision comparable to that of symphony musicians, destroyed ninety Syrian jet planes with no loss of Israeli life. This mission was accomplished with aircraft and machinery designed, built, and maintained by thousands of people who were almost all strangers to each other. This is organizational elegance extraordinaire.

The Apollo mission, discussed earlier, is in the same class. On that project, engineers and administrators deserve credit for doing their jobs well and being part of a larger social system that required superb socio-technical competence.

Moderate Cohesion, Low Complexity

The word *networks* refers to social relationships that, while stronger than one's presence on a mailing or telephone list, fall short of a group of friends. Networks are held together by shared values, which means that they are larger and more effective when the values that hold them together are cooperative and cohesive ones. Networks seldom have much structure other than a potential list of members. Organizations can't handle much complexity without adding structure, in which case a network would become something else, such as a club, association, or union.

How Networks Operate

A network is an understandable, viable, and useful niche organization. A network is useful for helping a group who shares commonly held values to provide mutual support and to pass on information relevant to those values.

The most recent uses of networks have been in business. In 1974, I started the first business network with a few friends. The network grew to over six hundred businesses that helped each other when mutual help was beneficial.

Our model was copied in Sweden in the late 1970s as part of a national policy to generate more small enterprises. Sweden was fertile ground, with a long history of cooperation and interest from both private and public entities. One third of all Swedish consumer purchases are still made at cooperative enterprises. The network project was successful over the six-year period I witnessed. Thousands of new businesses were started and thousands of established businesses learned to cooperate as a result. In fact, business cooperation reached a pinnacle, with networks bidding on large commercial projects including electronic manufacturing and shipbuilding.

The idea of the business network spread from Sweden to other parts of Europe, and reentered the United States in the mid-1980s with grants from the German Marshall Fund (a fund the Germans set up to mimic the original American Marshall Fund). Here the model expanded rapidly, starting, not surprisingly, in heavily Scandinavian-populated Minnesota and the Northwest, and spreading throughout the Midwest and central states.

Low Cohesion and High Complexity:
The Thanksgiving Marketplace

The annual American ritual of Thanksgiving, with the production, processing, delivery, and sales of millions of turkeys with little or no waste, would appear to be orchestrated by the miraculous invisible hand of the market. Not so. Similar feats of human cooperation occur all the time, with the complex structures behind such events invisible to us. With its tradition of specific foods, Thanksgiving affords little waste because the dictates of the tradition are stable.

Tradition acts as a form of cohesion. Roughly the same number of people buy turkeys each year and they buy them in the same predictable pattern a few days before Thanksgiving. Every business involved knows the schedule. Ads start running two weeks before, producers start ordering containers months before and growers start hatching turkeys many months before that.

On our chart Thanksgiving is on the lower end of the corporate ellipse.

An event of the same kind of scale and complexity as the Thanksgiving marketplace occurs every time there is a national election. National elections require coordination, cooperation, and a decentralized process. No one person nor agency announces the upcoming election and the necessary steps to have voting mechanisms in every precinct. The commercial marketplace, however, has relatively little to do with the election process.

Christmas, with its annual delivery of presents to adults and children nationwide, is a similar event to Thanksgiving and elections. The market plays a role, but so does almost every other social institution. The whole process is one of decentralized organization. Unlike Thanksgiving, however, Christmas produces a good deal of waste. Christmas merchandise frequently remains unsold, or is broken, unavailable, or returned to the seller. Christmas is based on gifts and individual tastes, which are not as clearly specified by tradition as the

Thanksgiving menu, so waste occurs. On our chart, the commercial Christmas would be close to but a little above Airline Passengers.

No Cohesion, Moderate Complexity

Automobiles on a highway would be found just below Airline Passengers. The reason traffic accidents declined as speed declined was because automobile traffic is a decentralized system where each driver is the autonomous operator. The skills of the individual driver substitute for an organization. As individuals slow down, their relative skills increase, and they can better cope with the stable but complex system outside their car. If driving had become more complex at the same time speeds decreased, (for example, radar-operated photo-speed-traps had proliferated) accidents would not have declined.

Cohesion and Complexity = Organizational Structure

All organizational structure is the result of the relationship between the two components of cohesion and complexity. Understanding the interaction of these two components will help us to better understand the nature of specific organizations.

If conditions require strangers to carry out a highly complex task, we know in advance that a tightly structured organization will be necessary to carry out exhaustive training of the strangers and that a highly developed infrastructure of support services will develop.

Conversely, given the structure, we can deduce the level of cohesion. If we know that an organization has only a few people managing it, with a large group of carefully trained part-time workers on call, we will also know that the organization has low interpersonal cohesion with moderate task-related cohesion. A Red Cross regional disaster office would be an example of this kind of organization.

Summary

Organizational structure governs society and is exemplified by team sports.

Organizational structure is often mistaken for the invisible hand of traditional economics.

Any organizational structure is made up of two components: interpersonal cohesion and task-related complexity.

Organizations with weak interpersonal cohesion range from strangers on a beach to airline passengers and the Thanksgiving marketplace. Organizations with strong interpersonal cohesion range from lovers to the Israeli Air Force attack on Syria.

Given these two components, an organizational structure will develop. If we understand the structure, we can identify the level of cohesion.

Industry Run Amok: The Snafu Society

The efficiency values of industrial society, with its emphasis on competition and resource optimization, have allowed systems-level errors to grow to the point where national productivity is harmed.

When large systems combine with over-zealous efficiency aims, the result is a snafu. The fallout is personal inconvenience and exasperation. Both are on the rise.

The word *snafu* originated in the United States Army during the Second World War. It is an acronym for Situation Normal, All Fucked Up. The dictionary meaning is "confusion or muddle"; the word can also be used as an adjective or verb.

Snafu is an important word that is worth some study. It does not simply refer to errors or mistakes. Despite the dictionary definition, confusion is only a small part of its popularly understood meaning. As native English speakers know, it refers to systems-level, or systemic errors: errors in the social system.

It is a snafu when you apply for a tax refund because the government made an initial mistake, and the refund check is made out for the wrong amount. It is a snafu when five people show up for a party to find no one home.

We live in a complex social system. *Snafu* is the only word we have to describe what happens when something in that system goes wrong. The wry humor inherent in the word is based on the fact that to be human in today's society is to have to deal with the fact that things will often go wrong.

Military Snafus

Just as it was in World War II, the military remains snafu-ridden. In the early 1990s Gen. Alexander Haig publicly criticized three major military operations over the preceding fifteen years as snafus on a large scale: In Iran, American planes and helicopters collided. In Grenada, massive numbers of United States troops landed without military opposition, yet American lives were lost. Targets were missed and a crew was lost when United States jets bombed Libya during the simplest of "practice" procedures.

The systems virus first recognized fifty years ago in the United States Army continues to plague our armed forces, and has spread to our consumer population and industrial society as well.

Consumer Snafus

We all encounter snafus on a daily basis. A credit card bill arrives, containing the same error you've spent three months telephoning and writing to correct. An ineffective auto repair creates a new oil leak, requiring visits to four supply houses for the right parts. A dry cleaner fixes one spot, but leaves a more noticeable one elsewhere on the garment. After the installation of a fire alarm, precluding the need for a separate tenant policy, a homeowner insurance policy premium goes up. The re-registration for a lost municipal bond costs more than the interest earned on the original lost bond because of a 1930s state law.

And just think what could be waiting on your desk today. An unsolicited gold calendar from American Express. (Try sending it back and getting it taken off your bill—hah!) Notification that a package has been mailed to your home, and no one's home to receive it. A request to mail a large box, requiring the right supplies and waiting in several lines at the post office. A note to yourself to get a new telephone line installed. Evident in all of these situations is error compounded with more error because of the systems involved. "Situation Normal . . ." would be better replaced by "Systems Normal . . ."!

Are Snafus Increasing?

Have snafus increased in the last several decades? And if so, is this increase in snafus affecting our commercial output?

I asked my friends about the first question. One, who regularly takes month-long trips for the State Department, noted that on her return, the time required to fix the mistakes that occurred in her absence has been increasing. She figures nearly two weeks of time is required to repair the damage created during a one-month trip.

Other friends pointed out an obvious measure: the amount of highway traffic and resulting traffic jams. Jam-ups have increased significantly in the past several decades, and very little is being done to solve this problem. Are there no solutions to this problem? Have we come to accept jam-ups as inevitable? Both answers are probably yes.

The best measure of the traffic problem is evident in my study of small business operations for my business consulting practice. When I study company records, I find that my clients make fewer sales visits and fewer product deliveries per day than a decade ago. That means that productivity has decreased in spite of improved routing and cargo handling. I've also found that the amount of administrative time away from work required by employees to handle personal problems has gone up significantly.

Measuring Snafus

The current main record of measurements in this country, the 1996 *United States Statistical Abstract*, is disappointing in its tracking of snafus. Out of more than fifteen hundred tables in the book, less than a dozen contain any relevant information about snafus, which are simply not being measured in the system as a whole. The "Situation Normal" syndrome seems to preclude the need to measure.

Only five tables in the Statistical Abstract clearly relate to snafus:

1. The number of people stopped and questioned while crossing the Mexican and Canadian borders: 6.8 million cars stopped in 1970, 10.8 million in 1980, 17.8 million in 1985, and 24.2 million in 1990. A big increase in a minor nightmare.

2. The number of motor vehicle accidents: 22.1 million in 1970, 24.1 million in 1980, and 32.5 million in 1990. With sixty million families in the United States, that means about one accident per family every two years. Look at the wasted time and cost for the countless people involved. Traffic deaths declined in the late 1970s because of the reduced speed limit. Why aren't more of us aware that accidents have increased steadily during the 1980s?

3. The number of business bankruptcy filings: 190,000 in 1970, 280,000 in 1980, and 725,500 in 1990. Imagine the wasted time spent straightening out all these messes.

4. "Restricted activity per capita," or workday disability: The number of days of illness or disability has risen from 14.6 days per working person per year in 1970 to 16.1 in 1991. The number of days of work missed for illness has remained steady at 5, so the rest of the sick time is occurring on weekends and vacations.

5. The number of lawyers: The figure doubled from 1970 to 1984, then increased by 22 percent to 800,000 in 1990. Unfair

jokes about lawyers proliferate, but that level of increase certainly reflects a corresponding increase in the number of snafus in our society. The increase could also be evidence of an increase in the kind of social problems that need mitigation.

Small claims court actions would probably indicate an even greater problem with snafus, particularly among people who don't use lawyers. Unfortunately, these important figures are not available.

Three Major Known Generators of Snafus

Three major changes in our society have made life noticeably more complicated in the past several decades: crime, working mothers, and single motherhood.

In 1965, we didn't have to lock outside doors or install home burglar alarms. We could enter downtown buildings without registering for a security identification card. There was no necessary sunset exodus from public parks.

Crime is now "Situation Normal." Crime figures increased drastically from the mid-sixties. On a yearly basis, there are now 2.7 million violent crimes, and 30.3 million other crimes such as theft and burglary.

By the early 1990s, crime began decreasing but citizens have not changed their mindset, the locks on front doors and automobile steering wheels are still in place.

Women with children have gone from 18 percent of the female labor force to over 64 percent. Surveys indicate that adult males in households with working mothers, however, have not significantly increased their share of the housework load.

Single motherhood has doubled as a proportion of the population from 1970 to 1985. Single motherhood is not only difficult situation for single mothers; it is also a burden for family and friends recruited to help with child care. Snafus seem to increase exponentially for single mothers and their stand-ins.

Different Effects for Different Incomes

The bottom economic stratum suffers most from snafus. Society tends not to work for people at this level in the first place. They can't get credit, jobs, buy houses, or avoid the daily threat of crime. Unfortunately, most single mothers are part of the bottom economic stratum.

The upper income stratum? They have more snafus than they want. After all, first-class travelers wait just as long on the runway as those who fly coach class. The difference is that the upper income stratum has private jets, chartered planes, secretaries, maids, attentive bankers, lawyers, and au pairs to handle snafus for them. The upper stratum controls the media and many political processes. You don't hear very much about everyday problems at this level, because snafus don't occupy as much of a wealthy person's time.

In fact, the freedom from snafus is one of the perks of wealth. The upper income stratum knows they are relatively protected from snafus, and they pride themselves on this isolation. Take the maiden voyage of the refurbished *Queen Elizabeth II* as an example. The cabin class customers were treated so poorly, they called a press conference to complain about the food, ventilation, service, and unfinished recreation facilities. When the press interviewed the first-class passengers, the typical response was, "Experienced travelers expect minor inconveniences." In fact the first-class problems were minor because major crew resources were devoted to minimizing them and the first-class passengers knew it.

It is the great middle-income stratum that seems to be the most recently and noticeably afflicted by the virus of snafus. The increasing incidence of snafus moves the middle-income stratum closer to the bottom stratum in regard to the level of difficulty experienced in everyday life.

The Astounding Costs of Snafus

Snafu data simply doesn't exist—no one is interested in collecting it. My educated guesses are made on the basis of the insurance industry's estimated costs of auto accidents and their careful calculations of related snafu costs. Direct auto accident costs have nearly quadrupled, rising from $23.4 billion in 1970 to $93.1 billion in 1990.

My calculations for the total costs of snafus, for one year, is conservatively based on the insurance companies' formula for determining the amount of insurance money paid out in an accident versus the real economic cost, which is one to three; that is, the amount of insurance money paid out in an accident is one third of the real economic cost of the accident. Insurance companies spend plenty of money on surveys to obtain accurate measurements, so this formula is fairly reliable.

The other half of the equation is based on the direct cost of the other snafus of daily life as determined by the *United States Statistical Abstract:* legal expenses, crime costs, non-auto repair costs, toxic waste spills, and lost days of work. The total of these figures is underestimated; because most are not reported. It excludes snafus involving credit, postal service, banking, all levels of government, and the health care system. Each of these areas is a nightmare in its own right, and each is—you guessed it—currently unmeasurable.

Multiply this figure by three, the standard insurance industry figure of actual costs of accidents versus the amount paid by insurance. Adding auto accidents to the non-auto snafu total gives us 20 percent of our total national civilian effort.

Twenty percent of our civilian output, or one fifth of our work effort, is used to correct or deal with snafus.

The Source of Snafus

What generates snafus in the first place? They are caused by one general error and three specific ones. The general error is our pervasive pre-industrial belief that competition is fundamental to business and that competition wisely manages the marketplace. This belief is inappropriate, as we will discuss in the next chapter. What is needed are specific institutions to remedy systems-level errors.

One of the specific causes of snafus is a careless work force supervised by poorly trained managers. Remember when American automobiles were so badly built they fell apart barely off the lot? As a result, Americans bought Japanese cars instead. American auto makers then imported Japanese cars and management to solve the problem. Has the problem been solved? Not entirely, but the quality of American cars is better now. The quality of American products from other industries, however, is almost as bad as that of cars two decades ago.

The remedy is for businesses to recognize their common need for workers who are as well trained as their Japanese, German, and Scandinavian counterparts. In these nations, labor is active in management and has strong union representation and a higher level of status than in the United States.

Businesses also need to find other remedies. A reasonable approach might be to retain the fluid labor market, but to create institutions that allow lateral transfers of workers. Health, retirement, and seniority benefits would remain in effect, as well as generous access to education and training.

A second specific cause of snafus is that competitive businesses and sloppy government agencies design their internal operating systems to protect themselves. As a consequence, the consumer ends up with the problems. Such businesses and government agencies make it almost impossible to get a refund, change a bookkeeping entry, or correct an error. Lack of response to consumer demands protects company money and assets, as well as bureaucratic prerogatives. Daily life thus becomes harder for the consumer, the person at the end of the marketing chain.

A few businesses are changing their behavior. They recognize that they operate on different principles, (discussed in the next chapter) and their clients are benefiting from the rapid recourse.

What is needed are institutions designed to remedy these problems. Such institutions range from truly effective better business bureaus to increasing use of policy analysis by legislative and administrative bodies.

A third specific cause of snafus is that financially based businesses systems are not connected and operate without regard for each other's effect on customers. The consequence is a deeply rooted Catch-22. (It's no surprise that the phrase *Catch-22* came from a World War II military story.)

For example, you need a credit card to open a checking account, but the credit card issuer requires a telephone number and six months on the job. The telephone company requires credit and a checking account. The job requires a telephone and a permanent home address. Renting an apartment requires credit, a deposit, and a checking account. Each separate system pushes its requirements back on the customer, without regard to the systems conflicts.

A rational system would create one special office and phone number that would have a carefully investigated collection of information, voluntarily submitted by the individual, that certifies the person's social stability, credit, work, and educational history.

Measurement, Measurement, Measurement

To remedy some of these nightmares we have to start measuring the problem. Then we have to look at other high-tech nations to see who else has the problem. Superficially, it doesn't appear that the Japanese have the problem at all. The Swedes, Swiss, and West Germans also appear relatively unaffected. All four of these nations have national incomes that exceed ours. Their growth spurts usually dwarf ours.

Then there's Britain. Their snafu level is worse than ours, and they refer to it as an incurable disease.

A solution to the snafu problem will be more difficult to find than solutions to problems of a careless work force and overlapping conflicting systems. All three factors require measurement. We need a National Snafu Index. To measure crime, the Justice Department already surveys 100,000 people over the age of eighteen on a twice-yearly basis. Snafu questions could be added to this survey.

As the seriousness of the snafu problem comes to light, the situation will cease to be regarded as "Normal." We will then move into the stage of developing policy remedies based on measurement.

CHAPTER FOUR

HONESTAS THE GODDESS OF CLIENTRY

HONESTAS, THE GODDESS OF CLIENTRY, SYMBOLIZES HONESTY
AND OPENNESS BETWEEN BUSINESSES AND THEIR CLIENTS.

Clientry

In this form of commerce, a business knows the names of its clients and pursues a lifelong relationship with them rather than concentrating on single sales. Reaching the mass market is not a concern of clientry; neither is market share. It aims instead for a long-term relationship with identifiable customers. This is achieved by offering uniquely tailored goods and services, not necessarily the lowest price.

All kinds of businesses have a client list that they work with for long periods of time. Boeing makes aircraft for a short list of airline company clients. Many other companies work only for government defense departments. Doctors, insurance and financial advisors, artists, hair stylists, and dentists often have long-term client relationships. It is the combination of a named list of clients and the goal of a life-long business relationship that defines a clientric company.

Identifying Clientry

Clientry is a new form of business; therefore, it is not easy to recognize it. To confuse the issue, some of the more advanced trading and industrial companies have adopted clientric practices, while many entirely clientric businesses do a very poor job. In addition, some businesses are a mixture of trade, industry, and clientry.

A business with a client list and the goal of long-term relationships is very different from a trader or an industrialist. Unlike the trader, the goal of a clientric business is not the individual sale. My auto mechanic has often checked out my car for noises that I hear or minor radiator problems and not charged me for the time. It's a lifelong business relationship, in which I bring him new customers and he gets all my repair business.

Clientry is also unlike industrialism, which aims for an expanding market share with the lowest production costs. The American Express card, the *Wall Street Journal* and the *New York Times* are examples of clientric companies. They all aim for a limited market segment and avoid the lowest-cost options. The American Express card is more expensive than other, similar cards. The *Wall Street Journal* and the *New York Times* are more expensive than *USA Today* and have much larger news collection staffs. All three companies serve a specialized clientele and work to maintain good client rela-

CHAPTER FOUR
HONESTAS

TYPE OF COMMERCE	GOD	BUSINESS GOAL	ASSOCIATED WORLD VIEW
Clientry	Honestas	Lifelong Relations	Openness

tions: Their toll-free calls are responded to immediately, and charge card and delivery problems are quickly nipped in the bud.

A few examples of clientry have been around for as long as a century: advertising agencies, family doctors, family dentists, and auditing firms like Price Waterhouse. Each has a list of individual clients with whom they try to maintain a lifelong business relationship.

Clientry Can Include Manufacturers

A company that makes a tangible product can be a clientric business. Boeing is an example, because it has a list of specific client airlines that it sells to.

The earliest manufacturing company to employ clientry was the Lincoln Welding Company. At the turn of the last century, Lincoln donated welding equipment to trade schools because they understood that the students who learned to weld with their equipment would be loyal, lifelong customers. Lincoln Welding is still around, and still offering a high-quality product.

Cross Pens employs clientry because it has always had a policy that their pens should last a lifetime and will replace one for free if it breaks or wears out. Neither Lincoln Welding nor Cross has a list of their customers, however, as a fully developed clientric company would.

The oldest clientric business category is probably merchant banking, for the object of these banks was to forge a lifelong business relationship with a limited list of clients.

What Clientry Is Not

Many businesses have a list of customers but are not clientric. Phone companies, utilities, and banks are examples, as are auto manufacturers who have a list of the people who own their cars. But the true goal of each of these companies is industrial efficiency and a large market share.

Some extraordinary trading businesses that take good care of their customers and think in terms of lifelong relations may appear to be clientric; Nordstrom is an example. Nordstrom is a fine department store company, but it is not clientric because many of its customers are one-time only and the company is happy to expand this one-time-only base.

Clientry Within Companies

Some companies have clientric sub-operations for particular clients. Phone and utility companies often have special divisions that focus on a small number of business customers, for whom they provide a customer representative. Similarly, banks have departments to focus on lifelong relations with trust customers and large corporations.

Running a Clientric Business

A clientric business can resemble an industrial business in that both may use long-term budgeting with multi-year projections. The difference is that the clientric business does not focus solely on cost cutting. It will have large budget line items for quality, innovation, and improvement, and treat profit as another line item, not the bottom line. Sales volatility will be controlled, not by firing employees who are highly trained, but by building reserves and carrying a large line of credit.

In dealing with clients, each relationship is of crucial importance to a clientric business. A single good decision can rarely increase business, because trust takes a long time to establish, but a single bad decision, breaking the trust, can be costly to the company. Great care must be taken to avoid losing clients. Budgeting, intelligence, and planning are vital.

Finding Clientry in the Yellow Pages

Distinguishing between trading companies, industries, and clientric companies may be best carried out by looking at real businesses in a real business environment.

Consider the following list of seventeen headings from the San Francisco Yellow Pages:

Contractors-Paving
Contractors-Pile Driving
Contractors-Pipe Line
Contractors-Pole Line
Contractors Referral Services
Controls, Control Systems & Regulators
Convention Services & Facilities
Convents & Monasteries
Conveyors & Conveying Equipment
Cookies & Crackers
Cookies & Crackers—Whsle & Mfrs
Cooking Schools
Cooking Utensils
Coolers-Evaporative
Cooling Towers
Cooperatives
Copper

A Yellow Pages listing is about as close as you can get to business reality. There are nearly 380 separate businesses in these seventeen categories alone, including many national and a few international ones.

Traders comprise eighty of the 380 businesses listed. Businesses based on traditional trade practices under "Convention Services" include listings for local print-copy shops, local hotels that depend on walk-in convention business, and a bus tour of the city. Under the "Cookie" listing most are retail bakeries, which are traders that depend on individual walk-in customers. The majority of the listings under "Cooking Utensils" are retail stores. In most of these cases, customers come in once and are not seen again.

Not all retail business is trade, however, because some unique stores, such as dressmakers, receive 60 percent of their business from repeat clientele.

Industrial businesses make up two hundred of the 380 listings. In the "Contractors" category, several contractors own large pieces of equipment that are cost-effective on large-scale jobs. They will take any customer, and they profit by having the most efficient large machine for the jobs they do. These businesses have grown to fill the geographic niche in their area. In the "Controls" category, nearly every business is an outlet for a large, specialized industrial manufacturer. Each control device or system is highly specified to a technical niche, such as the Fenwal thermo switch and automatic gas igniter. These pieces of equipment are made in low-cost, heavily equipped factories that distribute worldwide. The local outlets are the distribution part of industrial operations. Some of the cookie companies are also distribution outlets for production-line industrial operations, like Pepperidge Farms. The conveyor equipment and the cooler companies, like the control-systems companies, are distribution outlets for industry.

The copper companies are vestiges of the earliest industrial forms, not very different from their ancestors a hundred years ago. They take orders for a commodity that is produced in vast industrial quantities by global corporations.

Among these industrial companies are some that have clientric attributes. Most of the contractors work with the same clients over a long period of time. Many of the distributor outlets work with a limited number of repair workers and engineers, who are long-term clients. Industrial companies sometimes have clientric attributes in parts of their distribution system.

Slightly under one hundred listings out of 380 appear to be clientric companies. A few of the smaller contractors are really sub-contractors who work for a short list of general contractors with whom they have a lifelong business relationship.

Most of the convention services are small specialized companies that work with a client list for 80 percent of their revenue. These lifelong clients provide word-of-mouth referrals for the remaining 20 percent of walk-in revenues. Convention services include caterers, specialized tours, convention organizers, facilitators, display and exhibit experts, equipment rentals, and audio-video specialists. These are distinctly clientric because they work with a specific list of clients on a regular basis; they also act as sub-contractors for other clientric businesses involved with conventions who refer customers to them. For example, a convention organizer or facilitator will refer a client to an equipment rental shop; in this case the final billing may be the one-time customer, but the work is really of a sub-contractual nature.

The cooking schools service special-interest communities, and a good cooking school will maintain an alumni list and newsletters to sustain a lifelong business relationship with its students.

Scattered through all the categories are specially skilled workers, consultants, professionals, and technical institutions that are clientric; they have repeat customers and established reputations. Not all of them may understand the clientric nature of their businesses, not all may run their businesses well, and not all will be in the Yellow Pages next year; but they are clientric by nature, whether they know it or not.

There are ten listings that elude the trade, industry, and clientry categories. Convents and monasteries are not commercial at all, they are religious (unless, of course, they sell goods). Some convention centers and bureaus are built with public funds and are managed by government agencies for civic goals; they are governmental entities. The contractor referral service is an oddity because the client appears to be the public, but it is really the contractors, who created and pay for the referral service. It might be considered an association. I can't categorize the five names listed under cooperatives: a school, a Chinese family association, and three nondescriptive names.

The Five Characteristics of Good Clientry

A clientric business, when it is well run, has five distinct characteristics: recourse, team spirit, little advertising, cautious expansion plans, and transparent systems (especially the financial ones).

Recourse is the implicit and explicit message that recompense will always be made in the event of errors, omissions, and misunderstandings. Recourse is the touchstone of long-term business relations.

Recourse is vital. All businesses make mistakes, and misunderstandings always crop up over time. A common goal of many businesses is to reduce mistakes and misunderstandings, but reality requires that recourse must handle the ones that do occur. The customer must know that recompense can be made quickly, efficiently, and without rancor. That is good recourse. (For more on this subject, see my book *Marketing Without Advertising*.)

Having customer-relations personnel with the full authority to remedy errors and stop errors at the outset is a key element of recourse. It is also very rare in business.

Team spirit reflects the everyday working and operating environment for customers and employees. To ensure a good working environment, maximum authority must be delegated to employees with customer contact, which imbues employees with a positive attitude.

The clientrist's focus on lifelong customer relations requires an approach to personnel matters that is very different from the treatment of employees in industry. Both clientry and industry have a business world view of optimizing people resources, but clientry has a different calculus.

Because employees will remember if other employees are mistreated and because clients can react the same way, a clientric business will behave differently from an industrial business. The longer-term clientric approach to employees favors honesty, caring, and personal concern. Clientry has a strong commitment to keeping staff for long periods, including aging employees.

Advertising has little or no relevance for a company that has a list of its customers and seeks long-term relationships with them. Satisfied customers will promote the business.

Expansion is seldom considered important if it might reduce attention to existing customers. *Caution* is the byword for clientric businesses, which seldom make abrupt changes of policy. All changes of marketing and operations are carefully considered, along with client consultation where feasible.

Openness is the sine qua non of trusting relationships. A trusting relationship is at the core of long-term customer interaction. There are thousands of businesses that are completely open with their financial, personnel, and management data. (For more on this subject, see my book on open business practices, *Honest Business.*) In fact, this last distinguishing characteristic of clientry is also its essential business world view.

The Open-Door Policy in Business

Good clientry requires that business doors remain open physically, metaphorically, and behaviorally. The need for an open-door world view arises from the desire to establish lifelong client relationships. Such relationships are founded on mutual trust and the customer's recognition of competence in the business.

Both trust and recognition of competence are in turn based on honesty, or the known absence of deceit, and ready access to objective evaluations. This in turn favors openness in information and finances and developing organizational policies or structures to cope with the occasional lapses of mutual confidence, such as legally binding warranties, labor contracts, and consumer mediation groups.

Openness means giving the client all the information he or she needs to know about the product and the company. Openness means having public audits and publishing financial statements.

Imagine a clientric businessperson dealing with a lease negotiation. He or she would view the lessor as part of the business and wish to maintain friendly relations. The key elements in such a lease would be mediation provisions brokered by mutual friends.

Summary

The clientric businessperson, when confronted with a new situation, will bring to bear all of the ten business world views we have discussed.

He or she will ask: What's really going on here? How does the money flow in this situation? What is the evidence? What are the numbers? What are the rewards for everyone involved? What changes will it cause? What is the most efficient way to do this, including new ways to use materials and people? What are the organizational implications? And finally, the clientrist will always ask: How would this be helpful to my clients and how will it effect our relationship?

Competition: Where Trade and Industrial Values Collide with Clientric Values

Clientric businesses operate in the contemporary marketplace, where secrecy and competition thrive. How can clientry function with openness and honesty in this environment? Neither trade nor industry requires openness, nor is either inherently dependent on honesty.

What Is Competition?

The word *compete* comes from the Latin *competere,* meaning "to seek together," while the dictionary defines *a competition* as "a contest between rivals." The original meaning of *compete* emphasizes the unity of purpose behind a rivalry: Two or more people or entities who are seeking the same objective. In today's American business environment, however, the rivalry has fierce overtones, and winning is all that matters. Business magazine advertisements use phrases like "Kill the Competition" (Sperry Products); "Winning Is the Only Form of Competition" (Dataright); and "Number One is the Only One" (General Motors).

Even in sports, the ideal of a fair competition between relative equals, the original goal of the competing athletes of the ancient Greek Olympic games, has been replaced by the military metaphor of destroying the enemy and the Darwinian concept of the survival of the fittest.

In focusing on the goal of winning at all costs, instead of on the process of striving for the same goal together, we have changed the meaning of competition.

Businesses are organized into teams whose purpose is to help their company beat out others in their industry. CEOs are awarded millions of dollars for forcing their companies to the top of the heap in annual profits. The concept of killer-competition is justified as contributing to the common good by developing the best products and services, thereby eliminating weaker competitors from the marketplace This kind of competition, coupled with the proverbial invisible hand of the market, is considered the sign of a healthy economy and is supposed to motivate for workers to produce more, to lower costs, and to foster innovation.

Competition and the Marketplace

The majority of American business owners follow a killer-competition model of business. The devices used to follow this model are monopoly, manipulation, and secrecy. In "king of the hill" monopoly practice, similar businesses cannot compete because of exclusive sales agreements, patent protection, or legal exclusion. In killer competition by manipulation, a business will under-price or out-advertise others in the same field. And new businesses are routinely secretive about their strategy and tactics.

Monopoly, Competition, and Trade

Typically, retailers look for a location where there are no other similar stores. Killer-competition thinking tells them to aim for geographic monopoly. They often succeed, and thus do much less business as a result of their isolation from stores selling similar products.

Most people shop where the largest number of stores are clustered. The consumer believes the more similar stores the better, partly because consumers want one-stop shopping, but also because such a system allows for a greater variety of products. The best retail is usually in dense downtown locations or in large malls. Wholesalers do best who combine their outlets in wholesale marts. Locating businesses close together benefits everyone, and not because of discounts. Customers simply want to shop where the variety of selections is best.

This is the kind of competition that emphasizes the process of striving together, not the end result of being the only winner.

Monopoly, Competition, and Industry

For examples of industry monopoly we can look at the audio, video, and computer businesses.

In the 1950s, RCA developed the 45-rpm audio system and followed the killer-competition model. Unfortunately for them, their early-trader view of industrial commerce was no match for the clientric values entering the market at that time.

RCA tried to establish a monopoly position with exclusive records that could only be played on RCA-manufactured record players. They ended up with 100 percent of the teenage pop singles music market. And only that market. RCA got only one of many technically available markets at a time when RCA technology was superior to the rest of the technologies on the market. Audio professionals regularly used an eight-inch version of the 45-rpm records and loved them, but this version was never sold to the consumer market.

In the sixties, when the audiotape market was young, there were three audiotape technologies: reel-to-reel, eight-track, and cassette. Reel-to-reel was the product of the Ampex corporation. They chose a killer marketing strategy of monopolizing that technology, as did the eight-track developers. Cassettes were developed by Philips, a Dutch corporation that licensed its system to anyone who wanted it.

Ten years later, Philips was still receiving royalties from other producers and distributors in the audio cassette field. Cassettes had become the only popular form of audiotape, and Philips ended up still producing one third of all tapes sold worldwide.

When video recorders came along in the 1970s, RCA resurrected the same killer strategy that had failed with records in the fifties. They concentrated on producing their own proprietary equipment and performance material. Their video-disc recorder system failed inside of five years in spite of massive advertising. Sony, producer of Betamax, chose a less aggressive kind of killer-competition strategy, with limited licensing. Matsushita, the producer of VHS, adopted the Philips approach of licensing everyone who was interested in their technology. How many Betamax tapes do you own today?

The story of personal computers is markedly similar. Computer companies that were open about their designs, allowing other companies to make easy attachments, connect to their systems, and copy their models, thrived. Examples are the early Apple II models and IBM PC's with DOS. The killer competitors in the early phases of the computer industry wilted. They included Texas Instruments,

Motorola's Four Phase, Grid, and Standard Oil's Ampex, among many others.

Apple, Inc. moved to a monopoly strategy after the Apple II model and gradually became a minor personal-computer company as a result. The founder of Apple, Steve Jobs, tried the same monopoly model at his next company, Next, where it failed again.

Killer Competition with Manipulation

Many businesses commonly try to under-price and out-advertise others in their market, interpreting this as a successful kind of business competition.

The problem with this strategy is that it seldom drives others out of the market. Instead, it buys market share, usually for a short term at a very high cost. Many companies that tried this approach failed themselves after depleting their capital. Only a small percentage of companies listed in the Fortune 100 of 1955 are still operating companies today, and many of those who have dropped off the list tried to under-price and out-advertise their competitors. Examples are Singer Manufacturing, Cudahy Packing, Wilson & Company, Briggs Manufacturing, Philco, and Sinclair Oil.

Personal recommendations from existing customers are responsible for 80 to 90 percent of all new customers. Low pricing is only one element out of many that can lead a customer to the selection of a product or service. The exceptions to the power of personal recommendations are tourist businesses, products for soap opera watchers, and children's toys. In each of these cases advertising is important, but placing too much emphasis on advertising becomes a permanent high cost, because the other businesses don't disappear, they adopt different strategies.

Personal recommendations are based on a reputation for quality and service. How did you choose your last medical practitioner, travel agent, auto repair shop, day care center, or private school? Did a killer instinct play a role in your decision? I hope not.

There are numerous examples of killer competition working to effectively eliminate other businesses. Nearly all the examples when carefully examined, however, reflect the results of government intervention to quash other companies. Such is the case in the oil, steel, telephone, telegraph, shipping, banana, mining and utility industries.

New Businesses and Killer Competition

Some 80 percent of new businesses using the killer-competition model will fail in three years.

Businesses who reject the killer-competitive model at the outset are at a great advantage. Ninety-five percent of businesses guided by cooperation and openness are still in business after five years (see the author's book *Honest Business*). This success rate is not to be taken lightly by today's entrepreneur.

Such businesses welcome other new businesses in their field. They share information and resources. Because starting and running a business requires extraordinary skill and effort, new business need all the help they can get, including everyone from landlords, suppliers, and customers to other firms in their field. Openness attracts help, while secrecy drives it away.

Killer Competition and the General Good

Does killer competition, which we have so widely accepted in our business climate, actually benefit the common good in some way?

The metaphor we use for the market as a whole comes from Darwin, who himself borrowed it from Adam Smith (see Steven J. Gould's *The Flamingo's Smile* on this subject). We see killer competition as a form of the survival of the fittest, where poor products and companies are weeded out and superior products and companies survive.

Most corporate employees know that applying this biological metaphor to the marketplace is laughable: A Gallup poll showed that 80 percent of corporate employees think their company is poorly run.

Today's marketplace, with its mixture of trade, industry, and clientrism, has little to do with the biological metaphor. Instead it is more like a dish resting on a table.

The government infrastructure is the table. The government provides businesses with public-school-educated workers and a transportation system entirely subsidized in the form of streets and highways, as well as railroads, shipping firms, and airlines that were created by the government and are still heavily subsidized by it.

Government also provides police and fire protection, recreational land for employee vacations, and the primary retirement plan of Social Security. It also tempers anti-business pressure with a government-provided unemployment insurance system to take care of workers when business wants to cut costs or fire employees. (This point is made by the economist Robert Heilbroner in *The Nature and Logic of Capitalism* .)

The political view of the "free market" economy is thus an illusion. Tariff barriers for most products, tax subsidies for many (such as oil), and government regulation of nearly all others in the form of patent protection, the FAA, the ICC, the SEC, farm regulation, and billion-dollar-subsidies and price supports add up to a great deal of governmental support of the marketplace.

The marketplace is only a dish on the table of governmental support. Killer competition exists in the marketplace, but the whole system itself is based on cooperation, collusion, and reliance on the political process.

Killer Competition Isn't Beneficial to Consumers

All the evidence shows that killer competition does not benefit the common good in today's mixed commercial system.

Killer competition is what the big three American auto makers waged in the forty-five years from 1930 to 1975. These years are notable for a lack of technical innovation, safety features, and pollution control in the car industry. Only Volkswagen and the Japanese provided any innovative ideas. In so doing, they established enough of a foothold in a few big cities to fend off the killer industrial giants.

Most health innovations in the past century came about because of an improved sanitation system (developed by the government), nonprofit research labs, and university researchers. Most major technical innovations came from wartime military developments (funded by the government) and Bell Labs (a monopoly regulated by the government). The IBM 360 computer and many of its predecessors and successors were developed with funding by the CIA and other secret agencies. Two notable exceptions in the history of innovation were Thomas Edison, who operated before government funding was significant, and Xerox Corporation, which made effective use of a ninety-year-old process (xerography).

Major technical innovations have rarely come from killer-competitive companies. The great variety of developments, improvements, and variations in technology have come instead from the non-competitive environment.

The next time you hear a politician spout the rhetoric about competition and the free market being sacred in our society, I hope you will consider the metaphor of the small dish on a large table.

Summary

Clientry operates in a competitive business environment in which each business tries to develop and market the best product, not to destroy its competitors. The killer-competitive model is a dominant but misleading metaphor in business and economics. Killer competition fails in trade and fails even worse in industry unless government coercion is used to make it work.

Secrecy, another element of the killer-competitive model, doesn't work for new businesses, which need openness and help from many sources.

Killer competition also doesn't contribute to the society as a whole because consumers are victims of market restraint, and because this kind of competition usually doesn't generate significant innovation.

Clientric Economics

As clientric businesses become a larger and larger part of our economy, we need a new economic theory to explain and analyze them. Economic theory as we know it was created by Adam Smith in the eighteenth century in a purely trade environment and updated in the nineteenth century to deal with an industrial environment. But traditional economics doesn't work in a clientric world.

When businesspeople listen to economists, they sometimes compare the experience to a meeting with aliens. Why is traditional economic theory so disconnected from the contemporary business experience?

The marijuana business is a good case study to explain the weaknesses of traditional economic theory. Of course, marijuana is morally objectionable to many people; however, it is a commodity perfectly suited to a theory of trade, and I have selected because it is one of the few crop commodities that is not subsidized by the Department of Agriculture.

The marijuana business cannot be defined as an industry, because large-scale farming cannot be used to produce an illegal crop. Instead it is purely a trade good. The final objective of the seller is the individual sale.

Marijuana as a Test of Traditional Economic Theory

An ounce of marijuana cost $15 in 1963. Since then, the price has risen steadily. Today the same ounce costs approximately $250. Users report that today's marijuana is about twice as powerful as that of 1963, and inflation in the intervening years has risen by four times. Still, the rise in cost is significantly higher than economic theory would predict.

Factoring in the inflation rate over the intervening years would justify a price four times greater than in 1963, or $60 per ounce. Factoring in the increased potency should only double that amount for a total price of $120. So how did the price climb to $250?

The $130 difference between the current market price and the price that is predicted by traditional economic theory is strong evidence that this economic theory doesn't work.

Marijuana should be a clear and simple test for economic theory. It's pure trade. There is no other similar product on the market, therefore price substitution is not a factor. There's a large population of well-established buyers, and strong competition among producers and sellers. Marijuana is almost the economic definition of a perfect market.

In addition, the intervening thirty years have seen the introduction of three additional factors that should have lowered the price of marijuana rather than raising it: (1) The size of the market in the United States went from a few million buyers to tens of millions; (2) Production moved from overseas to domestic; with lower transportation and seizure costs (3) Criminal penalties dropped from a felony, mandating a twenty-year prison sentence for marijuana possession in many states, to a misdemeanor with a more lenient sentence in most states. Therefore, the price should not have gone up much. If anything, traditional economic theory would have predicted that marijuana should still be fetching $15 an ounce.

Any economist can come up with a rationalization for this anomaly. The rationalizations I have heard are convoluted. What good is traditional economic theory, held sacred by many, when it can't explain a widespread business that fits all of the theory's primary definitions: free market, price, demand, and supply?

The Building Block of Economics

The fallacy of traditional economics is in its core building block: the exchange of goods or services for a price, such as the exchange of a book for a price of ten dollars. All such exchanges over the period of one year, added together, become a total figure of exchanges. The figures can be plotted on a supply-and-demand curve. The curve has a supply side—all books published in the United States, ranging from 200 to 400 million per year—and a demand side of books sold. Traditional economics assumes that if the price of a book goes up, fewer books will sell. If the price goes down, more will sell. It turns out that the book market has seen dramatic increases in the number of books printed and distributed with a rise in the average price of books.

Most readers who aren't economists will find the following question ridiculous: Will more people buy book A or book B, if they are identical in size, shape and weight, and B is priced a dollar less? The question could only make sense for a commodity because books are not commodities, the content of the book is more significant than the price, much more significant.

Traditional economic theory, where price is all, originated in eighteenth-century Scotland, a trade-based society that worshiped price. The father of this price-focused theory was Adam Smith. Smith was a great genius, a Scot born several decades after his country lost its independence. He spent most of his life in Edinburgh with a few years at Oxford and in France, where he was influenced by the French Enlightenment.

Smith elevated two ideas to the pinnacle of Western thought. No one—not Marx, Einstein, Darwin, or Freud—has come close to proposing ideas that carry such weight in social thought and are as deeply embedded in American mentality.

The first idea is that exchange for a price is the basic building block of economics. The second idea is the invisible hand of the market, the concept that competition between individuals benefits the common good.

Today's Economics

Does exchange for a price work as a reasonable building block of economics in today's environment? The answer depends on whether you're a trader, industrialist or clientrist.

Stand behind an imaginary gas station, where a trader attempts to sell you a brand-new VCR. The model displays no identifying logos or language. How much will you pay for it? One hundred dollars? Fifty dollars? Make him an offer.

In the trader's car is a new copier. It's beautiful, but it sports an unfamiliar brand name.

The trader also proffers an office space for rent, at today's special low price. Make him an offer.

The questions you will ask yourself are not questions of price. The trader will gladly give you any of his three items for a low price; he has to. Without specific information, his merchandise is worth nothing to you. With the correct information, however, you might be willing to hand over a thousand dollars or more.

There is a lot of information you would want to know before agreeing to exchange money for the items or the space. What electrical voltage system does the VCR plug into? What tape formats will it play? How many scan lines does it output to a television? Where can it be repaired? Without this information, you could buy a VCR that would damage your existing tape library, and then you'd be looking at a negative price.

Technical information about the VCR, in this instance, is more important than price by a large margin.

As for the copier, without a repair contract or a maintenance plan, it is nearly useless. Repair and maintenance count for many times more than purchase price with any copier. And maintenance includes supplies. You may have gone to a flea market and seen perfectly good ten-year-old copiers for which supplies no longer exist. That's why they languish in flea markets. The day your "bargain" copier stops, money flows from your pockets to those of a repair person, who may not be able to fix it. The rush report sits on your desk, the staff scurries around looking for quick copy services or a replacement copier, and you have chaos.

Then there's the rental office. The price you'll pay depends on information about many relevant services. Is the office zoned for the uses you require? What about the lease conditions? Insurance? Access to telephone lines? Heating? Lighting? These service details could render a dollar-a-year rental offer too high to be appealing.

Transactions

In America, most commerce is no longer based on flea market conditions where you haggle over price and can't find the seller the next weekend when the product turns out to be defective.

Most transactions today occur in a semi-clientric environment where some semblance of an ongoing relationship exists. The smallest building block in clientric economics is a transaction, as opposed to an exchange. A transaction occurs in a "context" of commerce, such as a department store. The store allows for the return of unsatisfactory merchandise, such as a book with missing pages. Store employees give advice on the product and patiently answer questions. Price is a subset of a transaction, and the importance of price varies from all to none.

In a transaction environment, each transaction includes five elements: price, information, service, repair, and recourse.

Recourse is what happens when something goes wrong. The new roof leaks and the low bidder has moved to Canada, but Sears, good old reliable Sears, will come out and fix it. That's why Sears has over 50 percent of the residential roofing market, regardless of price.

We all know people who shop only for price. What happens when they buy off-brands or products and services without identification? Occasionally, when it comes to service, repair or returns, they get burned. Just as gamblers tend not to tally up the cost of their hobby, price-shoppers rarely reveal or consider the situations where a bargain has, over time, cost far more than the original purchase price.

How many price-shoppers are there? A recent *American Demographics* magazine survey reports that 76 percent of those queried would rather spend more on a high-quality product than save money by buying a cheaper one.

Transaction-Based Economic Theory

Conceding that the basic building block of today's economics is not price, but a transaction with multiple factors including price, what does that do to economic theory?

When the emphasis on price is replaced by other factors, traditional economic theory no longer applies, and the tactics of secrecy, killer competition, cunning, and product monopolization lose validity in the marketplace.

We shall look at each of these elements.

Secrecy

Traditional trade and industrial business theory valued secrecy about costs so that final sales could be effected at the highest possible markup.

As a result, government has passed laws to prevent secrecy from being used to trick the consumer. Laws prevent used-car dealers from turning back odometers and mandate open bidding for government contracts. Businesses and companies that are honest and open with their customers build up a fund of goodwill that is invaluable, while those who are exposed as dishonest often experience crippling losses.

Killer Competition

Today most essential goods and services are not affected by killer competition. We buy food and clothing, live in homes and apartments, and listen to records, read magazines, and tune to radio stations that are appropriate to our tastes and interests. Who chooses a doctor, dentist, hospital or masseuse for the most competitively priced service?

The consumer instinctively mistrusts killer competition. Businesses that stress their competitive nature, like credit jewelers and used-car lots, instill doubt in the buyer, who is then careful to make sure that preferred products, brands, and services are offered. Service and recourse are questioned and small print is actually read. The buyer may buy one item from such business, but will probably not become a regular customer.

Mass-market discounters like Home Depot and Circuit City (called "category killers") have instilled customer loyalty despite their emphasis on competition because they combine low prices with an extensive inventory of brand-name products and excellent recourse.

Cunning and Deception

Am I the only one who stays away from stores and merchants who have cheated me? Am I unique in avoiding tourist traps because most of their merchandise is junk?

Cunning may be still be considered a positive value in American business, but buyers, investors, and those seeking partners avoid it. Advertising is often deceptive in the United States, but similar patterns are not found in Scandinavia, Holland or Japan, three societies slightly more clientric than ours.

Transaction-based economic theory explains why cunning, which implies some level of dishonesty, becomes less effective in a marketplace with more clientric businesses.

In the simple commercial system of trade, cunning has a low cost. If a trader pawns off an oak table that is really painted pine, the buyer has not lost a great deal because the price paid was probably lower than it would have been in another setting. In a more complex commercial system, however, the cost of cunning rises significantly.

Would you fly in an airplane if you thought the aircraft manufacturers and airline companies were less than honest? Would you buy food, or medicine, or computer equipment if you though the manufacturer was untrustworthy?

How about baby food? When glass was detected in Gerber baby food, with the consequent bad publicity, the company sold out within six months of the media disclosure. The glass, which was within FDA size guidelines, was not the main problem; instead, it was Gerber's less-than-concerned public response to the discovery of the glass in the food. Gerber's behavior seemed more cunning than honest, and consumers lost faith in their product.

The Decline of Product Monopolization

Before the mid-1960s in the United States, consumers were used to product monopolization. We went to one store for Amana, another for Frigidaire, still a third for Kelvinator. We went to one store for RCA, another for Zenith, and a third for Philco. State-mandated "fair trade" laws kept that industrial marketing model in place.

The introduction of a large variety of imported goods brought about a decline of this approach, but many mass marketers still believe in it. They have their own stores and exclusive retail agreements to maintain their market. Marketers in this school of thought think they are getting a higher price for their product, based on their monopolization.

Consumers are now much more used to finding different brands of the same goods in one store, or similar stores clustered together in the same shopping mall. When the customer has choice, the customer is better served. The prices are not lower because of the product variety, for price is rarely lowered by proximity. An organic food store doesn't cut prices when the pesticide-ridden grocery store next door lowers its prices. A jewelry craftsperson located near a credit jeweler can maintain his or her own clientele— and charge prices considerably higher than the credit jeweler.

As market variety has grown, product monopolization has become less relevant to final consumers, who more often choose products for specific qualities. The tea drinker, for instance, will gravitate toward high-quality teas. Giant conglomerates buy out these specialized products in an attempt to corner every tiny niche and diversify. Why? Because their mass homogeneous markets, where product monopolization was possible, are shrinking.

There are two reasons for this, in addition to the availability of imports. As our lives become more complex, we require products and services with more information and more specialized connections to other products and services. An example of this increasing need for interconnection is found in kitchenware. Where we might once have used one pan for many cooking functions, we now rely upon a *batterie de cuisine:* one set of cookware for the microwave oven, one for the stove, and one for the grill, along with such devices as rice steamers, crockpots, and toaster ovens. Smaller, specialized businesses have sprung up to meet all of these needs.

The second reason for the shrinking of the mass homogeneous market is the availability of automated production equipment. Small businesses can produce smaller production runs of unique products at modest prices.

Economics Is Not Universal Across Cultural Boundaries

United States economists have never hesitated to give advice to Chileans, Nigerians, Indians, and anyone else who might ask for a loan from the World Bank. Every culture is presumed to have the same kind of economic system as ours, with a similar currency, interest rates, and trade regulations. Every society's economics is presumed to be based on a supply-and-demand curve that focuses on price minimization and profit maximization.

Transaction-based economics understands that, to the contrary, transactions in different cultures vary considerably. Some countries are 100 percent trade. Others are 5 percent trade, 20 percent clien-tric. The economic systems of these countries cannot help but differ from one another.

The elements of a Japanese transaction are the same as those of American transactions, plus one element not found in American business: status. Japan is a highly stratified society, beginning with the emperor, who is number one. Status is virtually unchangeable within the society. Most Japanese products and services are sold to minute status categories. The Japanese examine each product or ser-vice to see if it fits their social niche.

And one element of business also found in America is greatly emphasized in Japan, where recourse is taken for granted: Anything can be returned or refunded. To the Japanese, a dissatisfied customer is a business disgrace.

It should come as no surprise that the Japanese have a high pro-portion of clientric businesses.

French Recourse? Mais Non!

Interestingly, status also figures in French transactions. Like Japan, France is a highly stratified society. The consumer buys flowers and bread at outlets suitable to one's position in the social hierarchy.

However, the French transaction lacks two elements essential to the American transaction: recourse and repair. Recourse doesn't exist in France. A shopkeeper will say, "You bought it, you keep it. If you were foolish enough to buy it in the first place, it's your problem."

Repair is so rare in France that one seldom sees a choice of goods or services that are repairable.

Arabs and Trade

Arab societies are almost 100 percent trade. Unlike American, Japanese, and French transactions, credit is central to the Arab trans-action. What Westerners perceive as price negotiation is, in Arab markets, really a negotiation about credit.

The Arab seller invariably knows the credit history of the long-term buyer as well as that of the buyer's family. The final price can include compensation for past poor credit behavior, future risk, and the social power of the seller relative to that of the buyer. Almost all the other elements of the transaction, aside from status, and credit history, are minor. This occurs because the buyer-seller relationship is close to a monopoly it is rare that arabs change trading partners, they always go to the same store in the same souk.

That long discussion over coffee in the tent is about whether the buyer paid on time last week, whether the future marriage of a daughter might put the buyer's family in a financially precarious position, and whether the prospective husband will be a prospective customer.

As a consequence of different national elements of transactions, we should expect different societies to have differing economic systems. They do.

Forecasting Trends in the United States with Clientric Considerations

A predictable trend is the increasing number of small businesses. As buyers become more sophisticated and diverse in their tastes, the need for increased personal services and for more specialized products increases. Such businesses are necessarily small because service and specialization are inherently personalized; information is tailored to each buyer.

A countervailing trend favors national businesses in fields such as automobiles, copiers, and computers, where repair, maintenance, and recourse are vital. For buyers, repair, maintenance, and recourse are considered more accessible when dealing with a large company. Canon has repair outlets in hundreds of cities, as do major auto dealers and Sears. This is partly a reflection of a highly mobile society: When we buy a product that requires repair or maintenance and we don't know where we'll be when the product breaks down, we want to buy from a company that is represented in many locations.

Marijuana Redux

We are closing this discussion of economics based on transactions by returning to the earlier discussion of marijuana: Why hasn't the price of marijuana behaved according to predictions for a traditional economic trade good?

A big jump in price occurred in the late 1970s, when the United States government started dumping the poison Paraquat on the growing marijuana crop. The poison didn't reduce the marijuana supply to any great extent, but it did force buyers and sellers to form trust alliances. Buyers were forced to buy only from sellers who were known to be reliable and who could guarantee the absence of poison in their product all the way back to the grower.

Growers also became direct sellers in this period. The poison on the crops put a premium on a trusting relationship. Buyers and sellers moved away from a trade relationship to a clientric relationship that operated at a higher price level. Low-price sellers were driven out of the market for lack of buyers.

The need to form value-added chains of trusted people from the grower to the distributor to the buyer is what created the significant increase in price over the past three decades. The product was no longer a commodity, it became a pseudo-service, a chain of social trust.

Summary

The core premise of traditional economic theory is supply and demand converging in an exchange of money for goods or services.

In a clientric marketplace, the sale of goods or services is based only partially on price, and often price is relatively insignificant. Instead of a simple exchange, the sale is a transaction that implies a continuing relationship between the seller and the buyer.

A transaction-based economic theory is better suited to clientry than traditional economic theory, which is based on trade.

This theory replaces secrecy with openness, killer competition with competition for quality, and cunning with honesty.

As each national economy becomes more clientric, we become more aware of underlying cultural business patterns.

As a result of an increase in clientry, two trends are developing: we are likely to see more small companies and more national companies.

Jobs in a Clientric Business

In a clientric business, consequences are everything. If you make a mistake, you attempt to right the wrong or fix the mistake to the eventual satisfaction of your client.

An employee's ability to perform his or her job in any business is predicated on the knowledge of consequences and the ability to act promptly in good faith.

Business is slowly moving away from the world of trade ("Take this deal, or shove it") and industry ("Take this job, or shove it"), into the domain of Honestas. Here, the prevailing message is more like "Take this job (or deal) because it is mutually beneficial to our long-term relationship."

Job Satisfaction

What is one of the worst jobs you can imagine? How about an 800-number telephone operator, who sits at a computer in an Iowa warehouse, taking orders for magazine subscriptions from customers who are motivated by the television offer of a free Walkman with a new subscription?

This job lacks three different ingredients necessary for job satisfaction: control of pace, awareness of consequences, and security.

Pace Control

The control of time is essential to satisfactory working lives. If our schedule is tight and crowded with tasks and appointments, there is little time for creative input or for helping clients. A hectic employee is not a plus in a client-centered environment. Unfortunately, work continues to become more and more hectic today, and individuals determine their own pace less and less.

In today's work world, machines dictate our pace, our focus, and our timing. Computers, faxes, telephones, airplanes, automobiles—they all govern our daily life and have much to do with our job satisfaction.

If we measure the degree of pace control in a job on a scale from zero to ten, the work conditions of a dentist, crane operator, airline pilot, and truck driver all rate close to zero. A university administrator, management consultant, Tupperware salesperson, or minister are closer to ten.

When the job has a ten on the pace scale, the worker has time to reflect on his or her work, make improvements, and take the necessary time to remedy mistakes when they are found.

Awareness of Consequences

What are the consequences of any one individual's work? Will one factory defect in a piece of machinery result in an airplane crash? Will an imperfect software program cause a company to give its clients wrong medical advice? Will a policy decision based on a careless financial analysis result in the eviction of an elderly widow from her nursing home?

Most of us realize that we cannot always know the consequences of our actions. "Doing good" can sometimes have a bad result. If many consequences are impossible to determine, what can we do? All we can do is try to determine what consequences we can. The amount of knowledge we have of the consequences of our work is one way of determining the level of our job satisfaction.

Compare the consequence awareness level in the following two situations: In Situation A, you are a member of top management for a company that is destroying the environment by emptying effluent into a river. Your job is to review technical reports on the effluent and interrogate experts on the subject. In Situation B, you have a lower-level job that gives you no knowledge of the effluent levels or effects. Your employers assure you that the effluent is clean, and that company experts have given the river a clean bill of health.

The person in situation A has a higher level of awareness of the consequence or his or her job. Being able to see longer-range consequences allows you to monitor and change your behavior. Employees who are prevented by their employers from seeing the consequences of their actions can make decisions that can harm their customers.

Consequence and Management Structure

An employee's ability to see the consequences of his or her own actions increases in direct proportion to the openness of a business, the availability of management reports, the degree of decentralization in management, and the closeness of the business to its customers, community, and suppliers. These conditions also help to define a clientric business.

The ability to see consequences decreases in circumstances of secrecy. Secrecy exists where financial and management information is lacking, where the organization is highly centralized and hierarchical (such as the military or CIA), and where the workers are isolated from other workers, customers, and related peers involved in the final use of the product or service.

Workers with jobs that score high on the scale of consequence awareness are top managers who work directly with customers, dentists (because they see the consequences of their work), residential care nurses, and self-employed accountants. A low-level machine operator manufacturing an unrecognizable part in a secret project, a clerk who spends all of his or her time checking the signatures of check endorsements against signature cards, and a truck driver carrying unknown cargo for a large company rate close to zero.

Companies with job rotation, a practice that increases employee knowledge and experience, do well on the consequence scale, as do companies where a broad base of employees are involved in decision-making, and where employees deal directly with customers.

Security

The third dimension of job satisfaction is the easiest to understand: job security.

When conscientious employees see something going wrong in their work environment, those people must have the freedom to act positively or stop working, at their own discretion. If an action is going to cause untoward consequences for a client, then an employee deserves the right to inform management and request a change in that work practice. The employee also needs the option to do more research, and even to report such research to relevant people in and out of the company without fear of being fired or punished.

Job security is a dimension that measures individual freedom to exercise intelligent choice. If an employee can raise strong objections to working conditions and still retain his or her job and dignity, this freedom is obviously desirable in a clientric work environment both from the workers' and the clients' vantage point. If the employee can be fired for even the slightest questioning, then the job scores poorly. Today, nearly 50 percent of all United States workers can be fired on a boss's whim. Many more see their wages and opportunities for promotion frozen in retaliation for the slightest criticism.

I recall a farmworker who was directed to set the gauge on a pesticide dispenser far higher than was legal. After protesting to the field manager, the farmworker was told to get back to work. Knowing he would be fired for mentioning the subject again, the farm worker did what he was told.

On the security dimension alone, unions and the civil service, have traditionally been strong. Companies with grievance and internal appeals processes score high on the job security scale.

Worker-Client Relations

When the above three work conditions are met, the benefits extend to the customer and well as to the employee.

Employees who control their own pace can relate directly to the customer in a way that strengthens the client-business relationship. Consider the decades of telephone operators who had a strict eight-second limit on dialogue with customers and penalties for exceeding the limit. Is this customer service? Employees who control their own pace also reduce the rate of their errors, which ultimately impinge on the customers. Being able to determine the consequences of one's work obviously adds to one's pride in that work and in performing it well. Employees who can make decisions on how best to perform their job without fear of being fired are serving the interests of both the company and the customer.

Summary

In a clientric environment, mistakes are costly to a long-term relationship between the business and the customer. For employees to reflect this reality they need to be in control of their own pace of work, to be in an environment where they are aware of the consequences of their activity, and to know that when they act responsibly in the client's interest, they won't be summarily fired.

The Era Of Clientry

Here are five questions about clientry that will help to explain more about the nature of this form of commerce.

Is the Hierarchical Structure of a Clientric Company Different from That of an Industrial Company?

Rudimentary evidence suggests that the answer is no. But logic leads in another direction.

Many management consulting firms prescribe flattened hierarchies for large companies. It is popular to recommend fewer levels of management between the top and the bottom. Their reasons are twofold: to create a more flexible and responsive management, and to encourage the delegation of decision-making to a lower level.

Neither of these reasons follow automatically from observing the transition from industrial to clientric business. In fact, such reasons may come from a misreading of the trend towards clientric business.

The goal of a clientric business is to actively respond to the immediate and future needs of individual clients and to maintain an enduring relationship with them. This is done by rapidly adapting to changing client needs by correcting errors, and by anticipating difficulties. Such responses require autonomy of decision-making by even peripheral employees.

"Flattening" the existing hierarchy does not inherently facilitate employee autonomy. It may be possible for employees and departments to exercise greater autonomy, even when independent contractors are used, without changing the existing hierarchy. The issue is not flattening hierarchy for its own sake, the goal needs to be employee autonomy.

My experience suggests that a clientric company needs more hierarchy than an industrial company with the same volume of business. The more autonomous employees, exercising greater individual judgement in a clientric company, are more difficult to supervise. For example it takes one supervisor for four technical reps compared to one supervisor for eight production line workers. More supervisors per employee means more layers of supervision and more hierarchy.

The common way to avoid greater hierarchy in clientric businesses is to use more independent contractors (of high quality) and keep the business small in size.

Would a Clientric Company Have a Sales Staff Paid on a Commission Basis?

Commissioned salespeople are rare in trading companies. The concept of a commissioned sales staff took root and flourished in an industrial setting. Small-company trading environments don't foster specialization, which, while it may occur in trade-related production, does so on a very limited scale. The trader does most of the final sales work, and the necessity of protecting the gross sales margin does not allow much room for commission incentives.

The industrial environment is quite the opposite. The producer can have large excess inventories, which necessitate a sales force. Sales commissions make sense in this situation because the objectives are to get market share and to keep the production line moving.

The clientric company wants to serve the customer over a long period of time. What is the role of a commissioned salesperson in such a company? Can a salesperson who has focused on getting new customers as fast as possible also effectively gather information on the changing needs of those customers? Will a commissioned salesperson allocate the time to bring the customer into the home company to see what innovative accommodations can be made?

I'm reminded of a client in western England, a traditional woolen mill in a dormant industry. Industrial processes and scale of production had long ago forsaken this little company, and English woolen clothing is hardly in the vanguard of fashion.

The first marketing expert hired to advise the company on how to increase its sales recommended the manufacture of stylish fabrics that rely on fashion trends and big sales commissions. When that recommendation failed, I was their second hope.

After looking around the mill, I suggested that they change their focus from making fabric for clothes to manufacturing fabric for upholstery. Sales could then be made directly to furniture manufacturers without commission, and the company would incorporate clientric elements.

Furniture-company buyers were invited to the wool factory, which was housed in a twelfth-century castle on an impressive estate, and encouraged to advise on changes in the production process.

As it turned out, furniture-fabric buyers were able to order the exact fabric output that suited individual furniture manufacturers' uses. The intimate relationship of the fabric producer and the fabric buyer, each of whom had special technical needs, allowed fabric buyers to hone fabric production to suit the furniture producers' needs.

A long and close relationship developed with the new customers.

Will Clientric Personnel Practices Have an Effect on Society?

It is not unreasonable to expect consequences in society from the structure and values of primary businesses a century after those structures have taken root. By the 1950s, most Americans were part of some larger national mainstream organization, be it a church, Kiwanis, Rotary, Elks, Shriners, women's club, veterans' group, sorority, alumni organization, military reserve, or even a political party chapter. Joining groups was consistent with industrial society expectations.

Today, membership in such organizations is dwindling. Individual autonomy more closely resembles that of many clientric businesses.

Will the autonomous individual American of tomorrow be more clientric? Will he or she seek long-term interpersonal relations based on openness, honesty, and a public commitment to remedy errors and overcome difficulties? Will this change in business–customer relationships make us a more cooperative and compassionate society? It seems probable.

What Is the Role of Government in a Society with Many Clientric Businesses?

Americans don't really have much choice about the kind of government they get. The political debate rages over more or less bureaucracy and more or less centralized government—but not over the kind of government itself.

Government in America has grown from a seed to a great tree, in an ad hoc manner that creates laws, regulations, and benefits when and where we want them.

Most countries, with only a handful of exceptions, owe their government structures to emperors, kings, or princes. That makes American government structure unique and so autonomous that radical change is unlikely.

American government is already somewhat clientric in structure, just like many businesses that mistakenly characterize themselves as industrial (banks and utilities), but which are heavily clientric by nature (they know the names of their customers and could have them for life). Our government agencies (thousands of them) have an industrial outlook: They solve problems by hiring staff and growing in size, they reconcile policy conflict by becoming inefficient. (If they are given two contradictory policy goals, they do both badly.) The Immigration Service is a good example of this type of staff inflation combined with increased inefficiency. American business wants immigrant workers, but many other Americans want fewer immigrants, so legislation is contradictory; the INS grows larger and becomes more inefficient.

One thing we know about new clientric companies is that they step into niche markets where specialized information is needed. Clientric companies also dominate niche markets where tailored services are required. What this suggests is that small businesses can be expected enter the market for government services to provide the functions that existing government agencies are unable to provide.

These new businesses may be nonprofit or even specialized government agencies resembling water districts and downtown special tax districts.

Is the Clientric Company a Cause or a Remedy in a Snafu-Ridden Society?

A superficial view of the situation might suggest that the proliferation of small, poorly capitalized, autonomous niche companies might increase the level of snafus in our country.

Another view would see that many industrial companies treat customers in large clusters. They hardly know that individuals exist. Government agencies seem to operate in the same industrial mode. Unmoderated industrialism on a grand scale is more likely to be the real cause of snafus.

Consider this recent snafu told to me by a client whose business facilities were damaged in a flood. He repaired the damage in two weeks, with all the necessary approvals from his insurance company. The insurance company reimbursed him within one week of filing, but required two check endorsements from the Small Business Administration and the mortgage holder, a large East Coast bank.

Obtaining the two endorsements took nearly three months and more than a full week's worth of my client's top-management time. This snafu was caused by a government agency and a bureaucratic industrial company.

I believe it is more likely that clientric companies will emerge to solve snafu problems in the future.

An efficient service provider is one that duplicates a complex skill over and over. A private detective is a good example. A client calls about a suspected scam artist who is new in town. The detective creates a ten-page dossier on this scam artist and on delivery to his client, is paid five thousand dollars. Then, as the scam artist makes the rounds, the phone starts ringing with other clients, each wanting to know about the suspect. The private detective modifies the ten-page report slightly to suit each client and collects many more fees.

Is this a model of the way that snafus will be remedied in the future as more clientric businesses arrive on the scene? Will becoming expert at diagnosing recurring problems and reselling packaged solutions constitute the new method of snafu-solving in our society? Probably.

Is Clientry Economically Productive?

The economic wealth of the world did not increase very much over the many hundreds of years before the industrial revolution. It increased geometrically once industrial society began to emerge, however, and today it continues to grow.

The drive to reduce the costs of production and distribution is a primary source of economic wealth. It has created the economic wealth of the world we enjoy today.

Since clientry doesn't have cost reduction as a primary goal, we must ask whether it can generate wealth for a society?

I think the answer must be that clientry by itself does not generate wealth. In conjunction with industry, though, it can generate wealth by helping to reduce costs.

Like good government, clientry does this by helping to create a stable business environment. Good clientry provides technical, social, and other types of information and services to industry, which allows for better management, better decision making, and more insight.

Insight is a mechanism for reducing volatility in revenues for an industrial company and supporting economies of scale. An advertising agency can provide its industrial client with useful information on the changing tastes of consumer market segments and the changing nature of the communications media. If the agency does a good job, the industrial client will benefit.

Similarly an accounting firm can improve management controls and new tools for analyzing costs. The industrial firm can then apply those controls and tools to cost reduction.

Clientry does not generate economic wealth by directly reducing costs, but it can generate wealth indirectly in its symbiotic role with industry.

EPILOGUE

THREE TYPES OF BUSINESS

If you don't know how to classify your business in one of three categories, you have missed the point of this book. Commerce is a large domain that permeates nearly every aspect of our lives, but it is divided into three distinct categories. These distinctions are important if you are in business, they are even more important if you are running a business, and they are vital if you want to assess the impact of business on our lives.

The three categories of commerce are trade, industry, and clientry. Trade focuses on getting the right markup on each final sale, industry aims for price reduction through economies of scale, and clientry strives for lifelong relations with clients.

Because commerce has grown very slowly from being insignificant to being pervasive in the world (although the pace picked up in the last century), very little helpful thinking has been done about the nature of commerce. Commerce has displaced the imperial state, authoritarian religions, and invading armies, but the triumph of this slow-growing behemoth has obscured its tripartite nature.

Many business thinkers have recognized that there is a difference between trade and industry, and a few people have recognized the difference between industry and clientry. But in most cases the significance of these distinctions has not been appreciated. For example, the distinction between trade and industry has not been appreciated either by national development agencies such as AID in our own State Department or by international business.

American secondary schools teach that industry is based on economies of scale, but imply that when industry came along in the last century, it totally eclipsed older modes of business. It did not. Trade, its predecessor, continues. Trade is still growing in volume worldwide; in fact, trading companies handle several trillion dollars of business every year. Trade is the most common commercial experience consumers have, in the form of retail stores and restaurants. It has not been replaced by industry; instead, industry has created its own new and expanding world.

Trade needs no infrastructure, while industry needs a highly refined infrastructure of government, law, civil society and a long-term stable economic climate. Much of the world can thrive on trade, which does not disrupt traditional societies, yet international government development agencies and international businesses persist in trying to change these societies into industrial nations when they should be designing products and services that can flow through the ancient channels of trade.

If the correct distinctions were drawn between trade and industry, we would find hundreds of new products and services flowing into central Africa, desert Arabia, and Outer Mongolia, areas with few or no electric power systems, paved roads, or facilities to supply replacement parts or maintenance.

Traders can deliver goods and services to the far corners of the world, where they will be welcomed and appreciated. If we promoted trade instead of industry, we would not be fomenting rebellion and terrorism in developing nations. Trying to create a global labor force built around a forty-hour work week is not feasible in most of the world, and resistance to such a Western system is persistent. Understanding the distinction between trade and industry would allow government policy makers and responsible business-people to accept the status quo that has prevailed for millennia and isn't going to change any time soon.

The same is true for misconceptions about the nature of industry. For much of this century, corporate executives have competed to establish factories in developing countries. But industry is not trade; it requires highly refined governmental systems. Industry is not a weed that can grow anywhere; it is a hothouse orchid that blossoms in the environment of a highly refined and stable government. Watching corporations scramble to open offices in the disintegrating Soviet Union was sad. Seeing the same thing in China is sadder. The lessons of sub-Saharan Africa in the 1960s and 1970s, and of Lebanon, Yugoslavia, Iran, and much of Central America in the 1950s and1960s, were never learned. Industry is simply not possible without a stable government, and the legal structure and civil society such a government fosters.

The distinctions between industry and clientry are recognized by a few people, but many of the worst corporate and consumer nightmares arise because these distinctions are not appreciated.

One example is environmentalists being divided between those who believe business can be environmentally responsible and those who believe it can't. Another example is political activists being divided on whether and how to keep special-interest groups (businesses) from dictating government policy through unlimited campaign spending. Both of these political rifts arise from an erroneous analysis of commerce.

Industry is focused on cost reduction. There are many ways to accomplish cost reduction, ranging from technological innovation to marketing genius, but the two most common approaches are finding cheaper supplies (by destroying nature) and using government power to create private monopolies. By knowing this, we will know that industry is only concerned about the environment when faced with government-imposed incentives and penalties. In addition, we will know that industry will never stop trying to use the power of government to achieve its ends, regardless of the limits on campaign contributions.

Citizens become confused about these issues because clientric businesses, with their focus on lifetime client relations, are commonly supportive of environmental issues and quite comfortable with campaign spending limits. The behavior of a few clientric companies obscures the single-mindedness of industries. Understanding these issues requires recognizing the distinction between industry and clientry.

Corporate Executives Are Anxious

Many of the CEO's and corporate executives I know come to work most days secretly praying that they will survive, without calamitous problems, until they reach retirement. The world around them looks threatening, with hostile takeovers, costly legal battles, antitrust actions, defecting clients, managers jumping ship to join competitors, and daily newspapers featuring terrifying stories of corporate disaster.

If you are a businessperson, knowing whether your company is in trade, industry, or clientry can help make sense of your world. It can reduce confusion and alleviate much anxiety.

Knowing what type of business you have can make sense of the many daily decisions you confront. It can remind traders to focus on their gypsy qualities, those assets and skills that allow a trader to function nearly anywhere under nearly any condition and to focus on building a product line that has widespread appeal.

Knowing that your business is industrial and not trade or clientric can resolve dozens of perplexing daily issues. It can shape your research and development budgets, your marketing and promotion plans, and most important, your personnel policies.

Clientric companies need research and development that generates state-of-the-art quality, while industrial companies need R&D that extracts every possible cost saving out of every process. Clientric companies place their survival at risk by cutting personnel costs and by merging with new companies; industrial firms can do either with much less risk.

On the other hand, a clientric company can be confident knowing that its marketing budget is focused overwhelmingly on existing customers, while industrial companies must struggle to maintain market share and to keep from going into decline.

Knowing which kind of business you are in means knowing how to make decisions that will be effective, while seeing the world in a rational framework. Going to work each day may not always be fun, but it will become less anxiety producing.

Snafus

Coming home from a two-week business trip to face a backlog of e-mail, envelopes, and phone messages is likely to present the businessperson with one ominous message: SNAFU. We can be certain of regularly confronting snafus, those situations where the effort to correct an error will make the error worse and increase the loss of valuable work time.

Many articles are written and many TV exposes are produced about the snafus in our lives. Books on simple living are proliferating, but seldom do they explain why life has become so frustrating.

Snafus are the costly consequence of an increasingly complex society (America in a global environment) that has not developed mechanisms to mediate between the conflicting systems we have created. We are a complex society, but most of the conflicts between our systems (government, legal, bureaucratic, corporate, and civic) are left to the individual to resolve, either by wasting endless hours of time or by resorting to courts and litigation.

Clientric businesses will eventually emerge to help us cope with a snafu society, but we need to enlist every active resource we have to help with this problem because snafus are costly to our economy and well-being.

Fads and Social Sorting

Last year, one of the largest regional banks in my state merged with another large bank, and my business friends have been complaining ever since about the declining quality of service. As a former banker, I know that one bank had a top-flight operations staff, while the other had one of the worst operations staffs in the banking industry.

Maybe both banks needed to merge just to survive, but the combination of these two particular banks was terrible. If two universities as different as Princeton University and Arizona State University were merged, we know that the consequences would be lethal, with the faculties and staff sabotaging each other mercilessly. But somehow the merger of two equally different banks raised no eyebrows.

An understanding of the phenomenon of social sorting would make this type of situation much clearer and alleviate this kind of corporate distress. The same is true of the endless parade of management fads that CEO's and top managers face perennially. Every year sees a new management fad, from the "search for excellence" to the "one-minute manager." Understanding social sorting helps put these fads in perspective.

Corporate management has two serious problems: (1) understanding the nature of commerce and knowing which of the three types of businesses they are in; and (2) recognizing the inherent inflexibility of corporate personnel.

Every corporation is the end product of a long series of social sortings. Each employee who is hired and each one who leaves defines the character of the body of employees who remain with the company. As the number increases and time passes, the character of the corporation becomes more clearly defined and more resistant to change.

The need to change and the desire to change may both be great, especially as seen from the perspective of the board of directors and top management, but the potential for change remains minor. Hence the annual parade of management fads, each one promising to change the corporate environment, then slowly fading away.

There are only a few small ways that a corporation can change, and each of these requires an acceptance and appreciation of social sorting.

Gods of Commerce is an attempt to focus on and to clarify all of these vital points. It is the result of forty-five years in business, decades of observation, and years of careful thought. I hope it will be of use to all my colleagues.

THE END

BIBLIOGRAPHY

Beniger, James R. *The Control Revolution: Technological and Economic Origins of the Information Society*. Cambridge, Mass.: Harvard University Press, 1986.

Chandler, Jr., Alfred D. *The Invisible Hand: The Managerial Revolution in American Business*. Cambridge, Mass.: Harvard University Press, 1977.

Corn, Joseph J. *Imagining Tomorrow, History, Technology and the American Future*. Cambridge, Mass.: M.I.T. Press, 1987.

Douglas, Mary. *How Institutions Think*. Syracuse, New York: Syracuse University Press, 1986.

Gould, Steven Jay. *The Flamingo's Smile: Reflections in Natural History*. New York: Norton, 1985.

Hampden-Turner, Charles, and Trompenaars, Alfons. *The Seven Cultures of Capitalism: Value Systems for Creating Wealth in the United States, Japan, Germany, France, Britain, Sweden, and the Netherlands*. New York: Doubleday, 1993.

Hawken, Paul. *The Ecology of Commerce: A Declaration of Sustainability*. New York: HarperBusiness, 1993.

Heilbroner, Robert L. *The Nature and Logic of Capitalism*. New York: Norton & Co., 1985.

Hughes, Thomas Parke. *American Genesis: A Century of Invention and Technological Enthusiasm, 1870–1970*. New York: Viking, 1989.

Landes, David S. *Revolution in Time: Clocks and the Making of the Modern World*. Cambridge, Mass.: Harvard University Press, 1983.

Mintzberg, Henry. *Mintzberg on Management: Inside Our Strange World of Organizations.* New York: Collier Macmillan, 1989.

Moskowitz, Milton, and Levering, Robert. *The 100 Best Companies to Work for in America.* San Francisco: Addison-Wesley, 1984.

Olson, Mancur. *The Rise and Decline of Nations: Economic Growth, Stagflation, and Social Rigidities.* New Haven, Conn.: Yale University Press, 1986.

Sowell, Thomas, *Race and Culture.* New York: HarperCollins, 1994.

Weber, Max. *From Max Weber: Essays in Sociology,* Trans. by Gerth and Mills. Oxford: Oxford University Press, 1946.

GLOSSARY

Clientry: The practice of business where the object is a lifelong relation with known clients.

Commerce: The human domain of selling goods and services to others and the concern for the success of that practice. It is different from military, art, politics, governance, education and state. *Commerce* is synonymous with *business*.

Competition: Two or more parties seeking the same objective. The seeking can range from friendly to belligerent. The objective can range from trivial to significant.

Ganesh: The second god of commerce, Ganesh is the god of improvement. Belief in improvement is fundamental to progress which is a core idea of industry.

Honestas: The goddess of openness and honesty. Close relations require trust and trust requires honesty.

Industry: The outgrowth of trading that focuses on reducing costs by using economies of scale. This is accomplished through gaining a large market share, locating in stable societies, and seeking efficiencies in technology, distribution and customer relations.

Money: The form of communication throughout the domain of commerce. The application of numbers and specialized language to business transactions.

Recourse: The avenues available to a buyer to remedy dissatisfaction with a purchase. Example: one hundred percent refund and a sincere apology from the seller to the buyer.

Social Sorting: The mechanism in our society for individuals to become part of institutions: finding jobs, joining clubs, selecting stores, and choosing a place to live.

Trade: The worldwide practice of buying and selling goods and services for money. The object of the trader is to price each sale to equal or to exceed a standard markup that covers all costs.

Transaction: The focal point of all elements involved in a voluntary sale or purchase. The complete transaction can include information about the sale and provisions for future maintenance and buyer satisfaction.

Urbanus: The first god of commerce, Urbanus is a symbol of trade. Urban areas created trade.

World View: An understanding of how the world works. The perspective of daily life.

INDEX

A

Amsterdam, 5

B

Baptists, 39-40
Beniger, James, xii
bourgeois, xiii,32
Brasilia, 5
business world view, xii, 6, 8, 10-13, 15, 28-29, 32, 68-70
Byzantium, 5

C

Calvinist belief, xiv
Canaanites, 7
capitalism, xii, 2, 31, 36
Catch-22, 58
Chandler, Jr., Alfred, xii
cities, 5, 6-7
clientrism, xiii, 36
competition, 7-8, 16, 50, 56-57, 70-80, 83-85, 90
complexity, 42-48, 50
conviviality, 6-7
Corn, Joe, xii
credit, 7-8, 16, 19-20
culture, xiv, 2, 5, 9, 18, 20, 33, 78, 86

D

Damascus, 6-7
Danes, xiv
diversity, 6-7
Douglas, Mary, xii

E

Ebla, 7
economics, 50, 77-83, 86, 89
The Encyclopedia Britannica, 18

F

flag, 19, 36-37, 39-40
French, 2, 14, 26, 80, 87
Fulani, xiv, 1

G

Ganesh, xiii, xv, 23-24, 30, 33
Germany, xiv
Gomorrah, 7
Gould, Steven Jay, 75
Greek, 18, 71

H

Hampden-Turner, Charles, 2, 31
Hawken, Paul, xii
Hebrews, 7
Heilbroner, Robert L., 76
home, xiii
Honestas, xv, 90
Hong Kong, 5
Hughes, Thomas, xii

I

imperialism, xiii
India, xiii-xv
industrial, xii-xiii, 1, 9-10, 24-34, 50-51, 56
institutions, 6-7, 23, 45, 57-58, 67
institutions of tolerance, 6
inventory, 6, 84
Israeli Air Force, 46, 50

J

Japanese, 2, 11, 20, 26, 57-58, 76, 87
Jews, xv

K

killer competition, 72, 74-76, 83-84, 90

L

Landes, David, 31
language, xi, 6, 17-21, 81
Lebanon, 105
London, 5

M

Mali, xiv
marijuana, 78-79, 89
markup, 7-8, 15-16, 33, 83, 103
marriage, 88
Marx, Karl, xiii, 26, 80
Mediterranean, 1
mergers, 41
money, 10, 14, 16-21, 37, 40, 56, 57, 70, 81, 83, 89
Morocco, 8
Moscow, xiv

N

network, 46-47

O

Occam's Sledgehammer, 9-10
oil, 1, 19, 25, 51, 72, 74-76

Olson, Mancur, xii
organizationalism, 29

P

Philips, 72
practicality, 6, 12
price competition, 7-9, 16
profit, ix, xiii, 8-9, 17, 25-26, 37, 46, 64, 66, 71, 77, 86, 99

R

RCA, 72-73, 85
recourse, 57, 68, 82, 84, 87-88
repair, 7, 51-52, 56, 62, 66, 74, 81-83, 87-88, 99
rewardism, 14
Rockefeller, John D., 25

S

screen, 36-38, 41, 45
Singapore, 5
Smarland (Sweden), xiv
Smith, Adam, 75, 78, 80
snafu, 50-59, 99-100, 107
social sorting, 34-37, 40-41
sociology, xiv
Sowell, Thomas, xiv
striving, 71-72
Sweden, 5, 42, 138

T

Thanksgiving, 43, 47-50
Tilak, Bal Gangadhar, 24
time, 8-9, 12, 15-17, 19-20, 25, 27, 30-32, 34, 38, 40-41, 44, 48-49, 52-53, 55, 61-62, 104, 106, 108
tolerance, 6-7, 44
trade, ix, xii-xiv, 1, 3, 5-12, 14-17, 23, 25, 28, 31-34, 62-63, 65-67, 70, 72, 76-81, 83-87, 89-90, 96, 103-104, 106
transaction, 8, 10, 18-19, 82-84, 86-90
Trompenaars, Alfons, 2

U

Urbanus, xv, 6, 8, 16-17

V

Venice, 5

W

washout, 36-38, 40
Weber, Max, xiii-xiv
West Africa, xiv, 1, 6

ABOUT THE AUTHOR

Michael Phillips is widely listened to in the business world. As a consultant, he has advised the largest corporation in the world (a Japanese trading company) as well as hundreds of one-person businesses from Seattle to Stockholm to Katmandu.

Phillips has been a source of innovative ideas since his first job as a banker, when he organized MasterCard, created the first consumer certificates of deposit, and developed modern corporate cash management. In 1969, he became the youngest vice-president of a major American bank.

Later, as a corporate treasurer and foundation president, Phillips developed the first business network, which was organized in his hometown of San Francisco and spread rapidly to Europe. One of the cohesive network principles he introduced was open-books management, a concept that has since become widely accepted in corporate America.